Building
Authenticity

Building Authenticity

A Blueprint for the Leader Inside You

Todd Nesloney

Tyler Cook

ConnectEDD Publishing
Hanover, Pennsylvania

This publication is available at discount pricing when purchased in quantity for educational purposes, promotions, or fundraisers. For inquiries and details, contact the publisher at: info@connecteddpublishing.com

Published by ConnectEDD Publishing LLC
Hanover, PA
www.connecteddpublishing.com

Cover Design: Stacey Cook

Building Authenticity by Todd Nesloney and Tyler Cook. —1st ed. Paperback
ISBN 979-8-9874184-0-6

Praise for *Building Authenticity*

Building Authenticity is a call for leaders to live authentically, lead authentically, and impact our world around us through the life we live. Todd and Tyler share powerful, practical tools to develop ourselves into who we desire to be, so that we can lead where it matters most and leave a legacy that lasts. From our value systems to our relationships, this book lays the foundation for how to live and lead with authenticity at work, in our home, and throughout our lives.

> —Jon Gordon | 14x best-selling author of *The Carpenter* and
> *The Seed*

Todd and Tyler's new book has renewed, energized, and inspired me. What a wonderful contribution to organizational literature, and to those who aspire to live and lead with their heart, in service, faith, and in love. An inspiration for us all.

> —Sally J. Pla |children's author and advocate

The world is in desperate need of authentic leaders and *Building Authenticity* is the blueprint with a soul that can help guide the essential self-reflection necessary to take up the task. Throughout the book, Todd and Tyler offer frameworks, stories, and practical exercises to lead well, grow others, and give our best to a world in need.

> —Houston Kraft | Cofounder of *CharacterStrong* and author
> of *Deep Kindness*

Todd Nesloney and Tyler Cook's *Building Authenticity* is a refreshing take on leadership that emphasizes the power of authenticity. With its relatable stories and actionable tips, this book is a valuable resource for anyone looking to make a positive impact.

> —Brian Dixon | Author of *Start with Your People*, CEO of
> the hope*media network

Building Authenticity: A Blueprint for the Leader Inside You is exactly that...a blueprint. It is what every blueprint should be...clear, easy to follow, and exciting to implement. The stories will captivate you and bring you to the next page, but the practical application develops momentum for you and those you lead. From self-awareness to creating opportunities to lead, this book will help you develop the what, how, and when to move your team forward.

—Dr. Joe Sanfelippo | Superintendent, Author, Speaker

Authentic leadership is more than necessary these days for leaders to be effective. While leadership seems to be a vague and overused term, Nesloney and Cook provide practical tips and strategies grounded in research. In an era in which connecting with people is necessary, this book helps to unlock the power of authenticity.

—Neil Gupta, Ed.D. | Superintendent

Dr. Tyler Cook & Todd Nesloney contend that "there has never been a time when genuine, value-based leadership has been needed more than it is needed right now"—and they are spot on. *Building Authenticity* is a must-read for leaders! They not only build a framework for what authentic leadership looks like, they fill in every crevice with the latest research, vignettes, and reflection questions that will help galvanize who you are as a leader.

—Dr. Jill Siler | TASA Deputy Executive Director & Author of
  Thrive Through the Five

Where was this book years ago when I was a young leader? This is the book I've been needing! Todd and Tyler offer us something incredibly helpful and insightful with their book, *Building Authenticity: A Blueprint for the Leader Inside You*. Their words are a hopeful light guiding us forward to become not only better leaders, but humans. 10/10.

—Tanner Olson | Author and Poet, writtentospeak.com

In *Building Authenticity*, Todd and Tyler underscore that it's not only what we do as leaders that matters, but even more so it's about who we show up as on a daily basis that's important. From learning how to have the right mindset and interact positively with others at our places of work, to socially, to at home—they provide action items for all of us.

> —Steve Mesler | Co-founder Classroom Champions, Olympic Gold Medalist, Bobsled

This book is what leaders need right now as they are trying to be everything for everyone but sometimes lose themselves in the shuffle. *Building Authenticity* supports leaders in reconnecting with who they are and reflecting on what they bring to their teams. Filled with research, theory, stories, and practical application, this book will leave leaders refreshed, renewed, and refocused. Nesloney and Cook do a masterful job weaving their two voices to cut to the core tenets of effective and authentic leadership.

> —Allyson Apsey | educational leader and author

Todd & Tyler have consistently illustrated that our #KidsDeserveIt! Showing our appreciation for others requires developing authentic relationships. This book is a must-read for anyone that believes in the power of self-awareness, leadership, and connecting with others.

> —Sheldon L. Eakins, Ph.D. | Founder of the Leading Equity Center and Host of the Leading Equity Podcast

As a leader, you must be authentically yourself, no other iteration will do! You are you for a reason and within you are gifts, passions, and experiences that are uniquely your own. Your path to leadership is laid from your past and grown in the vision of tomorrow. I believe this book will give you food for thought, but moreover insight into your heart.

> —Troy Sikes | Associate Pastor at Brenham's First Baptist Church

We all gravitate to leaders who lead with passion—leaders whose sense of purpose flows from their abiding convictions—leaders with integrity. And this is the type of leadership inspired by Todd Nesloney and Tyler Cook in their recent book: *Building Authenticity: A Blueprint for the Leader Inside You.* This book is sure to resonate with both aspiring and practicing leaders who are committed to tapping into their own potential and expanding their influence.

—Danny Steele | Principal, Author, and Speaker

Building Authenticity: A Blueprint for the Leader Inside You is like a Leadership Retreat encapsulated into one book! There are many great leadership books that deal with leadership as a profession, but Todd and Tyler deal with leadership as a person, which preserves your humanity as you maximize impact on those you serve. This is a book of grace and growth for leaders at every level of experience. The depth and compassion of this project prove that empathetic leaders wrote this book. Get ready to become a better leader and an even better person after this reading experience!

—Hayward R. Jean | Founder, Speak Life Enterprises, Director of
Student Services, Orangeburg County School District

Todd's Dedication

For Liam and Brixton:
May you dream wildly, love big, and lead bravely in all that you do.

For Liz, the person I am today is because of your love and patience.
You help me become better every day.

Tyler's Dedication

First and foremost, to my wife Stacey.

Thank you for your wisdom, unwavering support,
and unconditional love.

You are the ultimate teammate.

For Elijah, Judah, Noah, and Anna.

I pray you would live out your calling with integrity,
courage, and authenticity. You were made for greatness.

Building Authenticity

Table of Contents

Foreword xix

Introduction xxi

Chapter 1: Answering the Call 1
    Authentic Leadership Matters. 3
    The Courage Within. 4
    Your Team Needs You 5
    Leading From Where You Are. 6
    The Process of Building Authenticity. 7
    Honesty and Grace 8
    Misconceptions of Authenticity 9
    Growth Is a Choice 10
    Next Steps 12

Chapter 2: The Blueprint for Authenticity 13
    The Research 13
    The Foundations 14
    Positive Psychological Capital 15
    Understanding That It Must be Developed. 16
    Next Steps 17

Chapter 3: Leadership Starts from Within 19

Self-Awareness. 20

Your "Dashboard" 20

"How Do You Experience Me?". 23

Self-Reflection 25

Get Your Mirror Out 27

A Pen and Paper 28

Your Quiet Place 29

Get Introspective to Gain Perspective 30

Closing 31

Next Steps 32

Chapter 4: What's at Your Core?. 33

Our Early Years 33

Identifying Your Values. 36

Your Values Put to the Test 37

Values Attract Values 39

Your Values in Action. 40

Next Steps 41

Chapter 5: Who Has Your Back? 43

Your Support Team. 44

The Value of Accountability. 46

360 Degree Feedback 47

The Johari Window. 49

Balanced Processing in Leadership 53

Closing 54

Next Steps 54

Chapter 6: It's Not Just About You **55**
   Untapped 56
   If Not You, Then Who? 57
   Gold Digging 60
   A Culture of Honor 61
   Examine Your Toolbox 63
   The Paradox of Personal Growth 64
   Your Life On Display 64
   The Trust Factor 65
   Vulnerability = Strength 66
   Next Steps 67

Chapter 7: Your Team, Your Culture, Your Opportunity **69**
   The Team We Build 69
   The Multiplication Factor 71
   How Do You View the People You Lead? 73
   The Uncomfortable is Worth It 74
   Water the Ground You are Planted In 75
   Relational Equity 76
   The Power of Empowerment 77
   80/20 Rule of Empowerment 78
   The Language of Empowerment 79
   Re-Writing the Leadership Script 80
   Next Steps 81

Chapter 8: Life by Design **83**
   Bringing Alignment 84
   The Value and Necessity of Boundaries 86
   The Priority Pyramid 87
   Your Plan Into Reality 98
   Next Steps 99

Chapter 9: Ground Zero–Your Most Important Leadership .. **101**

An Integrated Life 103

The Trap 104

Lead With Your Life 105

Build What Matters, Not What's Easy .106

Humility and Sacrifice 106

Family Values 107

Living Your Legacy 108

Closing 109

Next Steps 110

Chapter 10: The Role of Faith **111**

Servant Leadership–It's All About People 111

Our Value System 112

Our Source of Hope 114

Our Model for Integrity 114

Humble Confidence 115

Our Identity 115

Leadership and Faith in Today's World .116

Next Steps 117

Chapter 11: You Have What It Takes **119**

When the Going Gets Tough 119

The Cost of Authenticity 120

The Value of Self-Discipline 121

Positive Psychological Capital: A Deeper Look 122

When the Storm Comes 123

Why We Need Trials in Our Lives 125

Guard Your Heart 127

The Man in the Arena 128

Next Steps 129

Chapter 12: What Comes Next? **131**

TABLE OF CONTENTS

References 133
About the Authors 139
More from ConnectEDD Publishing 141

Foreword

By Hope King

Since the time that I was just a little girl, I always knew without a doubt that teaching was going to be my life's work. From playing school with my dolls to forcing my older, much more reluctant brother to be my student – my heart would come to life in that pretend classroom. Then as I grew older and some of those pretend schoolhouse dreams started to become realities, I vividly remember so many conversations when my career path would be questioned. "But don't you want to be an engineer; you are so good at math?" Or "Why don't you actually choose a career where you can make money?" Yet, when I would defend my passionate pursuit to become an educator, the conversation would always end with, "Well, then, you will, without a doubt, become a principal one day."

While I didn't argue those words out loud, the internal dialogue was a different story. Me? A principal? "No THANK YOU!" The thought of any kind of "leadership role" would instantly make me break into internal hives. That was never going to be my future. You see, at that point in my mind, a leader was someone in the spotlight. I had no space or desire for the spotlight in my world. But little did I recognize then that leaders—and many times the most influential and successful leaders—are often the ones in the shadows.

Fast forward to many years of being in the classroom when a little blog post skyrocketed my love for the classroom onto an extra-large and highly unexpected platform. Now I find myself leading an organization that reaches over 25,000 educators and over 1 million students every year. Jokes on me right? Me? A leader? (Don't worry the hives still come from time to time.) In this role, as I am working with other passionate educators, one of the biggest questions I often hear is about how they, too, can share their passion for teaching – from a stage, in a book, on social media. How can they lead? My honest answer to them is – you already are. You see, in our current world of analytics, algorithms, and follower count, we've lost our focus on the art of true leadership. And that's this:

Leadership isn't about leading in the spotlight. It's not about titles, followers, or accolades. Leadership, true leadership, is about leading in the shadows. It's about recognizing that leadership doesn't just occur from a stage, on a social media platform with millions of followers, or even from the chair of a highly sought-after title. Leadership happens even in the smallest moments of life. So all those years ago, when I refused to ever see myself in a leadership role, I was, even then, a leader. And you, too, whether you have self-selected the title or not, are a leader as well.

So, I want for you to stop for a moment before you dive into this journey to grow your leadership. What got you to this very place in life, where you, (yes...you!) are reading a book about leadership? What's the story behind your true influence? What are your stories of struggles or stories of strength that you can use to walk a journey with someone else? These very stories that we have walked in our own lives are what guide and, more importantly, influence our leadership with others.

Todd and Tyler are about to take you on a journey into reflective leadership in *Building Authenticity: A Blueprint for the Leader Inside You.* This isn't a time for you to define "IF" you are a leader. That's already been decided. Instead, it's a time and an opportunity for you to rise up and embrace the leader you already are within.

Introduction

You may have picked up this book and wondered if it was the book for you. You may have seen the word "leader" and considered whether you truly fell into that category.

So, before we even begin with this book we wanted to make one thing clear. You are a leader. Period. No matter your job title or role, you lead through the influence you have and the example you set. Eyes are watching you and ears are listening. You're a leader in your home, where you work, and within your friendship circles.

Now that we've hopefully helped make that more clear, let's dive a little deeper. We believe that *authentic* leadership matters. Because *who you are* is *how you lead*. If you had the courage to open these pages, you know that leadership is not for the faint of heart. True leadership—the kind that develops people into what they never even knew possible—takes humility, integrity, and unwavering commitment to the potential inside each person you lead. It takes understanding that failures and mistakes happen. Not to mention, that as you lead, you open yourself up to judgment and even ridicule.

But simply put, authentic leaders are true to who they are. In the face of adversity, they stand steadfast in their values. In the face of obstacles, authentic leaders infuse those around them with the hope and optimism to rise and overcome. And unlike leadership traits of the past such as charisma, self-interest, and fear-driven results, authentic leaders unite with vision, lead with purpose, and leave behind lasting legacies. Now, that doesn't mean that authentic leaders don't make mistakes or fall short sometimes. But it *does* mean that they're continually moving forward and are resolute in what matters most to them.

There is no denying that there are growing demands on leaders in today's society. Reading these words today you may very well be feeling the weight of these expectations on your own shoulders. You understand your responsibilities as a leader, but may be torn by the compromises you find yourself making when it comes to your personal life, your relationships, or even who you desire to be.

So, the goal of this book is to encourage you with the hope and possibility of not only leading as your best self, but also giving your best self to those that matter most in your life. Leading authentically starts with living authentically, and this book's aim is to cultivate self-awareness, awaken fresh vision, and embolden you to live a life of prosperity through being true to who you were created to be.

As we will unpack throughout this book, there is power in authenticity. When leaders live and lead as their most genuine, authentic self, people around them see the same potential inside of *themselves*. Furthermore, authentic leaders have the ability to cultivate trust and develop sincere relationships with those around them. Because of this trust, authentic leaders can then awaken and develop those they lead towards *their* fullest potential in life, too.

This is the privilege of leadership. And it is through these lenses of authenticity that this book is written.

CHAPTER 1

~

Answering the Call

You have greatness inside of you. It is inside all of us. That simple truth we know without a doubt. You can feel it come alive during those times when you are living as your "best" self. When you know you're doing exactly what you were called to be doing at that very moment in time. We all know the feeling—there is something invigorating when we feel like we are firing on all cylinders; when we are leading change, bringing out the best in others, and all the while being true to ourselves. When it all just seems to be falling ever so perfectly into place.

It is in these moments that we truly tap into our *authentic* leadership. When we serve as our complete selves and have the deepest and most lasting impact.

The narrative is simple: The call for authentic leadership is greater than ever. We need leaders in our homes, businesses, schools, churches, and government who live from a place of values, transparency, and humility. Leaders who are willing to make the *right* decision, even when it is the *hard* one or one that few agree with.

According to the most recent Edelman Trust Barometer (2022), 77% of Americans say that knowing a leader's personal values holds importance in building trust. However, only 46% of Americans actually trust their leaders and institutions to act in a moral and ethical manner.

In our society today, organizations long to find leadership that will restore confidence, hope, and optimism, while displaying resilience in the face of challenges. They desire a way of leading based on character rather than charisma, and integrity rather than position (George, 2007).

We believe it is truly heartbreaking that less than half of Americans actually trust their leaders to simply do what is right. But guess what? You have what the world needs! Yes, *you* have what it takes—to develop a culture in which the *vision* you foster makes no room for *division*, and where relationships truly matter. A place where people feel valued, believed in, and appreciated. Because when people feel valued and appreciated, they will go beyond expectations and strengthen the culture of your team and their impact.

You have this potential inside you, and our sincerest hope is that you are awakened to move towards becoming not only the leader you have always dreamed of becoming, but also becoming the spouse, parent, and friend that you desire to be as well. Because after all, that is your true legacy. To lead, and lead well, in each area of your life.

Authenticity plays a critical role in today's world, as those entrusted to lead others have the responsibility to do so in a manner that not only adds value to their organization, but also to the people they lead and serve. Clapp-Smith et al. (2009) stressed the urgency for leaders to be transparent, to have an awareness of their own values, and to guide organizations with a moral and ethical perspective, in order to provide hope and vision for all stakeholders. As a result, research has found that authentic leadership consists of these characteristics and processes—both as leadership qualities and personal lifestyles of those leaders.

Insight from a fellow leader: *"For me, authenticity is a nuanced and evolving thing. But more than that, it is a relationship. In other* *words, I don't see it fully existing apart from the people and environment a leader serves. To be fully manifested, authenticity needs to be reciprocal. In a personal and/or professional sense, this means that in order for us to show up as our authentic selves, we need to create the conditions for others to do the same—which requires grace, reflection, listening, growth, feedback, trust, and an honest acknowledgement of the strengths we see as well as opportunities for important growth and conversation. In a spiritual sense, authenticity requires ongoing and honest connection. With ourselves. Our creator. And the work He wants to do in us and through us."*

–Brad Gustafson, Principal and Author

Authentic Leadership Matters

When Alan Mulally was named president and CEO of Ford in 2006, the famous American automaker was on the brink of bankruptcy. The company was preparing to post the biggest annual loss in its 103-year history: $12.7 billion. However, in less than a decade as CEO, Mulally was known for leading one of the most impressive corporate turnarounds in history and was eventually named #3 on FORTUNE's list of "World's Greatest Leaders" (Fortune, 2014).

When describing his leadership style, Mulally said, "At the most fundamental level, leadership is being authentic to who you are, thinking about what you really believe in and behaving accordingly. At Ford, we have a card with our business plan on one side and the behaviors we expect listed on the other."

Whether you are leading a local non-profit, a Fortune 500 company, a church, a group of children, or your family at home, you have an opportunity to live out your values in every interaction, decision, and circumstance. When you stay committed to your value system and embed it into your leadership practice, it is like a tide that raises all ships. It becomes the standard by which your organization and the people in it operate. Who you are as a leader should be so woven into the fabric of your organization that your team knows your response to a moral or ethical dilemma before even asking you. There's your sign!

There has never been a time when genuine, value-based leadership has been needed more than it is needed right now. Societal, legal, cultural, ethical, and bureaucratic pressures exist at an all-time high. But, you have the ability to write your own story. You have been entrusted with influence, wherever you are in life. No matter the sector, demographic, or size of your leadership footprint, you have the opportunity to live and lead from a place inside of you that is fortified by values, self-awareness, and identity.

The Courage Within

During Tyler's doctoral research (Cook, 2020) on authentic leadership in educational leaders, he interviewed a school principal who discussed the importance of making decisions when faced with moral and ethical crossroads. "*I preach all the time, no matter what staff I have, that whatever decision you make, there are always two paths. You can do the easy thing, or you can do the right thing. I always base my decision on the right thing. It has always, for the past 16 years of leadership, never let me down. It's not always the easiest thing in the world, but it is always worth it*" (Cook, 2020, p. 101).

When you live with authenticity, you are guided by your own "true north," not your present surroundings. It is courage in times like these that not only moves your organization forward, but helps build this same capacity in the people you lead.

As leaders, this "true north" must be what shines through in difficult times in order to foster collaboration and engage people, committing them to a common purpose. There is a sense of urgency that has risen for trustworthy, authentic, and transparent leaders to create cultures in their organizations and personal lives that embody these same values.

But, leading this way isn't for the faint of heart. When we lead with authenticity we allow others inside our world. As we become vulnerable and transparent, we open ourselves up for feedback that we might not necessarily want to hear, but really need. This can undoubtedly challenge us in uncomfortable ways, even shining a spotlight on areas in which we need to grow. But you know what? We believe that as the saying goes, without risk there is no reward.

The reality is that whether you're leading or following, there will always be the possibility of failure, heartache, mistakes, and disappointment. Instead of fearing what might be, why not lead as our most authentic and genuine selves and find ourselves surrounded by a team who walks beside us in the sunny *and stormy* weather?

Your Team Needs You

We have all been there. We have worked or served in organizations that lacked purpose. Lacked a sense of "team." A job that never valued what we brought to the table. Somewhere we felt invisible or easily replaceable. An environment that *lacked* a culture that encourages vulnerability, transparency, and risk-taking for the sake of the team's growth. A place where we felt a leadership void.

As you know, the characteristics of healthy organizations require intentionality; they do not happen by chance. Unfortunately, some people work their entire careers in environments that require simple compliance over growth and innovation. These people aim to please their boss and meet their quotas, without ever realizing their true potential. What a tragedy! As leaders, we must catch hold of what we are really here for. It's more than meeting the bottom line of our companies. It's more than managing the x's and o's of the job.

As Ann Fudge, CEO of Young and Rubicam said, "All of us have the spark of leadership in us, whether it is in business, government, or as a nonprofit volunteer. The challenge is to understand ourselves well enough to discover where we can use our leadership gifts to serve others. We're here for something. *Life is about giving and living fully*" (George, 2015, p. 9).

Have you ever felt like you were made for something more? That there was untapped potential deep inside? At some point we all feel the spark just like Ann Fudge says. We were ALL meant to lead. To inspire and grow others.

Leading From Where You Are

As leaders, we are all at different places in our journeys. Some of you may be new to leadership. Feeling like you are still "in the fire" of learning how to cast vision for those you lead, empower those around you, meet the demands of your organization, etc. Others of you may be seasoned in leadership, with years of rich experience that was formed by lessons learned and mistakes made along the way.

Additionally, some of you may not be in "formal" leadership positions, but instead realize and understand that you have influence in the relational spheres of your life and areas that you have been entrusted with. If that is you, let's make one thing clear—you are NOT just a mom, just a dad, just a teacher, just a student, just a college kid, just a friend, or just an employee. You are created to impact the lives of those around you. Who you are *matters*. The life you live has the potential to change the trajectory of others.

This is integral to the foundation of this book. Regardless of your title or season of life, you have the privilege and responsibility to lead where you are with love, confidence, and authenticity, for the sake of those around you. In your family, your organization, and *your* world. There is an authentic leader inside you, and this is the blueprint to discovering and developing it.

The Process of Building Authenticity

Authentic leaders show up every day for those they lead with their best, fullest selves. Their most authentic selves. If you are wondering what that truly looks like, or even how to get there, it is important to understand that it is a daily process. Authentic leadership is not a place where a leader has "arrived" at, but rather it is a process on a continuum that must be cultivated daily. It is a process whereby one day you feel like you've mastered it and yet the next feels like you're starting over again from scratch.

However, it is not about a "fixed point" in your life. Other leadership theories emphasize that you are either born with the characteristics of a leader or you are not. It's not about "charisma," and it's not about getting someone to do what you want them to do. It's not about being an introvert or extrovert. Authentic leadership is about living and leading with values and transparency, giving a voice to others, empowering teams, staying open to feedback, and infusing hope, optimism, resilience, and courage into every situation and every person. It is about staying true to who you are, while awakening others to who they truly are.

> Leadership development begins with personal development because who you are is how you lead.

As you read those words, you may be thinking, "If I lead that way, won't people walk all over me?" Or, "That sounds terrifying to open myself up to others." Or, you may even be thinking, "But I am not wired that way."

And that's OK. As a matter of fact, it *does* take vulnerability and it *does* take courage to lead with authenticity. It takes *work*. But the reward of strong relationships, organizational trust, and a powerful culture of empowered people is worth the cost of vulnerability or leaning into being uncomfortable as a leader. Your people are worth it. And the peace and fulfillment that you will experience as a result will be worth it as well.

Throughout this book, we will unpack the core tenets of authentic leadership, and the foundations of what it means to live and lead as your most authentic self. Things such as:

- Identifying your core values
- Establishing healthy support systems in your life
- Welcoming trusted feedback
- Living from your priorities
- Building powerful and empowered teams
- And much more

Honesty and Grace

As we embark on this journey together and you engage with the components of this book, remember to do two things:

1. Have honest, objective conversations with yourself.
2. Have grace for yourself.

Without an honest, objective evaluation of what drives you, what is important to you, and even your weaknesses, it will be difficult to cultivate *true* authenticity. After all, the goal is about becoming and growing into the person you desire to be, for the sake of yourself, those you love, and those you lead. The goal is not to become someone you believe others want you to be. If you aren't *honest* with yourself and even willing to make *uncomfortable changes* in your life, it will be difficult to bear fruit and find the subsequent peace at the heart of true authenticity.

Then comes the work of having grace for yourself. You may catch yourself feeling discouraged by all the ways you have not stayed true to your values in certain situations or fallen short of your own expectations of who you desire to be. You may doubt your gifts. Remember, this is a journey. Your courage to even read through these pages represents your commitment to grow–to do the stuff that most people aren't willing to do.

Part of any growth in life is to feel the sting of dissatisfaction with our current state, and the resolute nature to not stay there. To pursue a more preferred future. So, if you don't like where you are at or if you are feeling stuck–*don't stay there*. You have greatness inside you, and it's closer than you think.

Misconceptions of Authenticity

Let's be honest, many of you have heard the term "authenticity" in a number of contexts over your lifetime. Unfortunately, this word has gotten a bad rap and has even been misappropriated in many ways. We see people use the word authenticity as a free pass to not use a filter or to "speak their mind," in the spirit of being their "authentic self." It is used as a thin veil to lack tact, empathy, emotional intelligence, or justify their unwillingness to engage in healthy, respectful discourse.

For example, people may say, "*I am going to start speaking my mind. I owe it to myself to be true to myself,*" or even "*I was just being honest.*" Though those statements may be true in some sense, we want to pursue a different type of authenticity. An authenticity that is a pursuit of becoming your *best self.* Your ideal self. Just because you can do something or want to do something, doesn't mean you should. That is literally the antithesis of what we are after.

Building authenticity is about identifying your ideal self and becoming that person you desire to be–what you stand for, the values you desire to embody with your behaviors and decisions, the way you love and impact people, and how you foster healthy, transparent relationships in your life. It's about identifying who you *want* to be, and then committing to *live intentionally* each day in pursuit of it. Living a life defined by purpose, integrity, and impact. A life that builds a legacy worth remembering.

Other times, we have seen people or society use the word "authenticity" in a context of compromising morals and masking poor decisions with being "the real me." Again, such an unfortunate representation of the goal and foundation of this powerful word. As the saying goes, *"What is right is right, even if no one is doing it, and what's wrong is wrong, even if everyone is doing it."*

As people of character—leaders who are passionate about loving and leading with lasting impact—we have an opportunity to truly define what it means to be an authentic leader. A leader who sets the standard of morals, values, relational health, and living a life of example for every path they cross. That is what we are after, each and every day.

Growth is a Choice

We have all been there. Watching a fitness clip or listening to an inspirational speech. Having a conversation with a successful person we admire or even reflecting in a moment of honest introspection about our life. Whatever the moment looks like or emotions that are evoked, we have all caught a glimpse of who we *could* be. Who we *want* to be. Our *potential.*

For some of us, it drives us to passionately pursue this vision at all costs. For others, we doubt our ability to get there, even though we know it is inside us. We even sometimes convince ourselves that we could never be like that. Some of you may feel like you are behind the eight ball in life. Or perhaps you feel that you have made mistakes leading in the past, and it's too late to change the culture at work or home that does not currently look like you want it to.

Wherever you find yourself today, that's OK. Nothing is too late, and no one is beyond redemption. Just as the old proverb says, "The best time to plant a tree was 20 years ago. The next best time is now." *Your time is now.*

That being said, regardless of where you are in your journey or on the spectrum of building authenticity and the leader inside you, the same is true for all of us: *Growth is a choice.*

Growth does not happen by accident. It takes intentionality every day. It takes grit. It takes commitment to keep our compass on the horizon ahead of us and our crosshairs firmly fixed on our target. Unencumbered by distraction, and unwavering to any voice besides the ones that truly matter. It takes the ability to understand that just like a field or forest must be burned to allow new growth, so we must endure some cleansing to reach our full potential.

The truth is, you have tremendous potential inside you. Potential to impact the trajectory of the lives of those around you. Potential to leave a legacy for generations after you. Not simply as a result of what you do with your life, but *who you are.* However, potential without action is just that: potential. The very definition of the word potential is: *Existing in possibility. Capable of development into actuality* (Merriam-Webster, 2022).

Those are powerful words, and the best part about it is that you have everything inside you necessary to become the person you desire to be—*If* you are willing to do the hard work on the inside. The humble work. The type of work that opens you up to feedback you might not want to hear, but will result in your exponential growth. The type of work that requires second chances, forgiveness, and apologies. But if you're ready, the work is worth it. The people you lead are worth it. Your family is worth it. *You are worth it.*

So, as you read through this book, sit up a little straighter. Posture yourself in a way that recognizes the potential inside you. Sink your teeth into the vision you have for yourself, your life, and your leadership, and don't let go at any cost. Then, create habits, routines, and mindsets in your life to build on each previous day and foster your growth. When you do this, you will not only build authenticity in your own life, but you will also set a standard and model a blueprint for those around you to do the same. In fact, research by Luthans and Avolio (2003) found that those who live and lead with authenticity actually impact those around them in such a way that others begin to identify with their own values, traits, and authentic selves. It creates an ecosystem in which authenticity can be cultivated in others. Talk about a powerful, value-driven culture in every sphere of your life!

Growth is a daily choice, and one you are capable of making. You were destined for greatness, and this is a part of your journey. So, onward, and upward we go.

NEXT STEPS:

1. Think about your life through the lens of your *influence*. Who is in your sphere? Is it your family, friends, co-workers, congregants, etc.? List the groups of people, as specific as possible. Begin thinking about the opportunities you have to truly impact your world around you by the life you live and the example you set.

2. What limiting beliefs, if any, do you have about yourself as a leader? Be honest with yourself. Throughout this book, we will be unpacking keys to growth and developing yourself into the authentic leader you were created to be.

CHAPTER 2

The Blueprint
for Authenticity

The Research

So, what exactly is authentic leadership? What does it truly mean to live and lead with authenticity? Well, we are glad you asked. Since our goal is to help you build a solid, lasting foundation of authenticity, we are going to go back to the foundations of authentic leadership theory. That's right, not just an opinion in an article that you read online, but actual researched-based fundamentals of what it means to be an authentic leader. It is from this framework, our own research, as well as our own lived experiences as leaders, that serves as the foundation for the concept of this book.

As you have (hopefully) perceived in the opening pages of this book, authentic leaders are defined as individuals who know who they are, what they believe, and are aware of their own and others' values, knowledge, and strengths. They are aware of the context in which they lead, and are confident, hopeful, resilient, and of high moral character (Avolio et al., 2004). They generate trust and develop sincere connections with those around them. Because of the trust that is cultivated, authentic leaders are able to motivate and inspire others to elevated levels of performance. Additionally, they are morally uplifting, driven by shared values, and empowering to those they have been entrusted to lead (George and Sims, 2007).

In application, authentic leaders act upon deep internal values, interact with those they lead to build trust, foster relationships, and lead transparently. Through high moral standards, integrity, and honesty, trust is built, and organizations can flourish (Gardner et al., 2005). Doesn't this sound like a leader you want to follow? A leader you'd want to become?

The Foundations

The word "authenticity" can be traced back to ancient Greek philosophy, which instructs individuals, "to thine own self be true." This mirrors a similar ancient Chinese phrase, "to square one's words with one's conduct" (Avolio & Gardner, 2005).

Authentic leadership consists of four main components:

1. Self-awareness
2. Relational Transparency
3. Balanced Processing
4. Internalized Moral Perspective

More specifically, Walumbwa et al. (2008) suggest that leaders with more *self-awareness* continually seek to grow and develop themselves because they know their weaknesses through self-reflection and introspection. *Relational transparency* refers to presenting one's genuine self in all situations and circumstances (Walumba et al., 2008). *Balanced (unbiased) processing* refers to the objective analysis of information and involvement of stakeholder's perspectives in decision making processes. Finally, an *internalized moral perspective* refers to an established sense of behavioral integrity and consistency between values and actions based on internal moral norms and values.

Individuals who lead with authenticity are those who act in accordance with deep personal values and convictions, build credibility, win the respect and trust of followers, and genuinely desire to serve others through their leadership (Avolio, et al., 2004). It is through these lenses and from these underpinnings that we build authenticity in our lives and leadership.

Positive Psychological Capital

Authentic leadership has also been found to play an important role in the development of positive psychological capital in those they lead and those around them. (Luthans & Avolio, 2003). What is this technical term? Positive psychological capital is defined as an individual's positive psychological state of development, characterized by the amazing characteristics of:

1. Hope
2. Optimism
3. Resiliency
4. Self-efficacy

From a leadership standpoint, positive psychological capital has been shown to have a powerful effect on employee engagement, job satisfaction, organizational climate and psychological well-being at work (Avey et al., 2011).

This means that your positivity, your belief in others, and even your resilience when the going gets tough is actually *contagious*. How wild is that? When you live and lead from this place of hope, optimism, resilience, and self-efficacy, there is a mirror effect that takes place. It models and helps build this within your team, your family, and those around you. Which therein only leads to greater things.

> **Insight from a fellow leader:** *"One can't lead others until they can lead themselves. To quote the late great Vince Lombardi, "Leading by example isn't the best way to lead, it's the only way to lead." My focus on leadership is bettering myself every day. I do this by constantly seeking critical feedback from my team, reading books written by/ about other great leaders, constantly challenging myself to do things that will make me a better person."*
> –Riley Feldman, Managing Partner

Understanding that it Must be Developed

Just as we shared in the previous chapter, authentic leadership research indicates that building authenticity and becoming an authentic leader requires a commitment to growth and taking responsibility to develop oneself. This is contrary to the idea that leaders are born with a specific set of characteristics or skills that stand them apart (Avolio, 2005). Bill George, author of *Discovering Your True North*, asserted that authentic leadership is birthed and cultivated through the life stories, experiences, and personal narrative that helps one find their true identity and how they can add value to their world around them (2015).

From practicing their values, to finding balance in life, to empowering those around them, authentic leaders foster growth on a daily basis and are willing to use their experiences to become authentic in all aspects of their life. This idea also embodies Carol Dweck's research on mindsets (Dweck, 2006) which showed that those who believe they can change their basic beliefs and attributes are more likely to persevere through challenges and failures. It is through this level of self-awareness and self-reflection that leaders are able to develop greater depths of authenticity, and in doing so, become better leaders.

So, no matter your leadership capacity or context by which you influence and impact those around you, you have the ability to build healthy, genuine, and impactful environments allowing those around you to thrive. The calling on your life and the greatness inside you isn't meant to just stop with you. It is meant for your world around you, from those at work to the next person you engage with after you look up from the pages of this book.

Now that we have established the foundation of what it means to be an authentic leader, let's dive headfirst into how you can build the life, leadership, and legacy you desire from the *inside out*.

Insight from a fellow leader: *"Being genuine toward your core values allows a leader to focus on how to take action without being sidetracked. All leaders encounter obstacles and challenges, but a stringent focus on what truly matters allows them to model making things happen. Not just talking about it, but being about it. In other words, saying what you mean and meaning what you say."*
–David Domena, Elementary Educator

NEXT STEPS:

1. When looking at the four positive psychological capitals discussed in this chapter, (Hope, Optimism, Resiliency, Self-Efficacy) which do you find yourself lacking in and why do you think that capital has fallen below the others?

2. What steps do you need to take to grow in that area? (Growing aware of how you respond to challenges, fostering a growth mindset, being cognizant of which inner thoughts you listen to, etc.)

CHAPTER 3

~

Leadership Starts from Within

The world around us is full of noise. Pressure to perform. Expectations to conform. Even mixed messages about who we should be, how we should behave, what we should think, and the words we should say (or type). One glimpse into the messages today's society sends out can be as slippery a slope as Frodo sliding on the "One Ring" in the Hobbit.

If we are not grounded in who we are, what we stand for, and our values as leaders, we are vulnerable to the subtle slide of trying to live and lead from an unhealthy place. This could be the validation from others, pressure from our careers, or even compensating for our own feelings of inadequacy and need to prove ourselves. Regardless of the reason, it is now more important than ever that we cultivate two extremely important practices in our lives: *Self-Awareness and Self-Reflection.*

Insight from a fellow leader: *"In every decision I make, I depend on what I have gone through and the perspectives/suggestions of my team. My team at work are my fellow leaders and my team at home would be my wife. As a leader, I want those I am leading to*

know that my stance and decisions are not knee-jerk, but thoughtful. Ultimately, as a leader, I work to be authentic by not asking anyone to do a thing that I would not do myself."
–Leonard Galloway, Principal

Self-Awareness

Simply put, self-awareness is defined as: The ability to see yourself clearly by recognizing and understanding your moods, drives, and emotions, as well as the impact you have on others. Furthermore, it is the process whereby we continually develop an understanding of our own talents, strengths, weaknesses, purpose, core values, beliefs, and desires (Gardner et al., 2005).

> **Insight from a fellow leader:** *"I would define authentic leadership as a leader I would want to follow. A leader who actively listens consistently and has integrity. Approachable is another word that I find in a great leader. I love a leader who isn't afraid to go against the norm and do the right thing."* –Stephanie McConnell, Principal Principles

In Daniel Goleman's groundbreaking book, *"Emotional Intelligence"* (EQ) (2005), he notes the five dimensions of EQ: self-awareness, self-regulation, empathy, motivation, and social skills. Unlike our IQ, research has found that it is possible to grow in EQ, which takes discipline, courage, and humility.

Your "Dashboard"

Have you ever been driving in a vehicle and something feels "off"? Or have you ever had a check engine light go on in a vehicle you were driving? You instantly become keenly aware of every rattle, shift, and nuance of your ride. The dashboard of your vehicle serves the important purpose of indicating the "health" of the many facets of your vehicle. It would be foolish for us to ignore the flashing lights on the dashboard of our car, knowing it might lead to a more costly issue down the road. Yet many of us are guilty of ignoring our own personal dashboards and flashing warning lights.

Imagine attempting to drive across the United States on an important road trip—one with purpose and meaning. However, before you leave the house, you decide to place electrical tape across the dashboard of your car. No clue of your fuel level, speedometer, or even tachometer. Sure, you will be able to feel your way through the first couple hundred miles, but after a while, you are certain to find yourself in a troubled spot.

Our lives consist of high-stakes leadership positions, teams to steward, and, most importantly, our families who rely on us, and we often push ourselves to the "limit" by ignoring our fuel gauge, speedometer, tachometer, or even worse—our check engine light. What's worse is that we do it in the name of "sacrifice" for those who mean the most to us. Yet, little do we realize that we are in fact not giving our families the best version of ourselves, but rather one that is drained, short on patience, or even disconnected emotionally. It hurts us and others more than it actually helps.

> Great leaders make sure their families & friends get the best of them, not the rest of them.

Pushing ourselves beyond our limits without cultivating self-awareness isn't noble at all. In fact, it pulls us away from the person we desire to be, and into someone who finds themselves surviving, rather than thriving. A person others can't rely on or trust. Furthermore, it could place us in a moment of weakness that could even compromise our morals or values. True self-awareness is about knowing a *healthy you* vs.

an *unhealthy you,* and then understanding what is needed to recalibrate so that you can bring your best self back into the game. In the end, if you can't take care of yourself, how are you ever going to take care of anyone else?

A Story from Tyler

One key to fostering self-awareness is to understand the health and proportion of our responses to situations. For example, if I find myself in a conversation with my wife Stacey and having a disproportionately large internal response to a seemingly casual conversation, it is an indication that I need to look *inward*. More often than not (let's be honest, probably 95 times out of 100), it is something inside of me that I need to lean into and assess, rather than the present situation.

In these situations, I have found that the simple internal phrase, "I'm going to *get curious* about that" turns my attention from the external situation to my internal response. Once I am able to identify more clearly what the trigger is, I am better able to take the next steps to find victory in that moment and beyond.

As it relates to work, I find it generally easy to see the best in others and extend grace when needed. However, in moments when I feel criticism creep in, more often than not it is a lack of clarity, peace, and health on my end of things that shortens my ability to love and lead those around me the way I desire to. When I focus on the *internal* work needed inside of me, I become more empathetic, passionate, and visionary. I then have the internal measure to show up with my whole self for the people I lead and care about.

"How Do You Experience Me?"

Another aspect of self-awareness is the ability to look humbly and objectively at how our moods, emotions, and decisions impact those around us. This is by no means an easy task. In fact, it can be a scary thing to realize how the people in our lives *actually experience us*. We have our perceptions of how others view and experience us, but without trusted and honest feedback, we could be missing the mark without even knowing it.

We will discuss the value of relational support systems later in this book, but it is vital that we welcome trusted people into our lives who are willing to provide us honest feedback. 360-degree feedback. The type of feedback that even *they* know will go down like a bitter pill, but will be good for us in the end. After all, why would we want to fool ourselves into thinking that we have no areas in which we need to grow? In reality, the more humble we are in asking for feedback, the more grace those around us are likely to show us, aiding our growth in the process. We must make sure our circles include people who will tell us:

+ No
+ Are you sure?
+ Have you thought about it this way?
+ That was inappropriate

We must have people in our lives who will push back, challenge, and therein make us better. All from a place of love.

When 75 members of the Stanford Graduate School of Business Advisory Council were asked to identify the most important capability for leaders to develop, their answer was overwhelmingly, "self-awareness" (George et al., 2007). In regard to leaders, George et al. (2007) went on to acknowledge that the ability to know one's authentic self requires the courage and honesty to open up and examine their experiences. As they do so, leaders become more human and willing to be vulnerable.

In leadership, we generally are surrounded with people who are used to saying "yes" to us. However, if we want genuine, open feedback into how others experience us, those people need to be free to share beyond the comfortable or what they think we want to hear.

In a work setting, a survey is a standard and easy way to gather feedback. However, the downside to a survey is the lack of relational engagement, resulting in sometimes unproductive feedback that does more harm than good. Surveys can also be highly skewed to how people feel in that exact moment (like when given at the end of the year) instead of how they have felt with the year as a whole. Instead, one great way is simply an intentional conversation with those around you. Perhaps one that you cast a vision for prior to the discussion.

A primer for the days leading up to the conversation could be, "It is important to me that you are experiencing me in a way that communicates clarity, care, and compassion. I am looking for honest feedback on how I can better serve our vision together and support you. Please come with any ways that I can refine my approach and strengthen our relationship. My goal is to grow into the best leader for our team that I can be."

If you have not done this before, people you are serving may hesitate at first. But, after they get over the initial "awkward" hump of telling their leader the ways they are experiencing them, *and* seeing that you actually follow up and respond to their feedback, you will see the level of trust and impact of your team grow in powerful ways. Not simply because you are fostering self-awareness and taking intentional steps to grow, but also because you are now modeling a culture of open and honest feedback. When modeling comes from the top, real and lasting change begins to happen.

When leaders are willing to humble themselves and grow, it creates an environment where others see the value and safety to receive feedback, take risks, and pursue their potential. It's time that we no longer let fear, pride, or insecurity limit our growth or the growth of those around us.

> **Insight from a fellow leader:** "*When we lead authentically, we are true to ourselves and our morals and values. It's playing on our strengths while acknowledging and working on our shortcomings. It's about celebrating our successes while owning our mistakes and striving to make amends.*"
> –Todd Schmidt, Principal

Self-Reflection

Over the past few years, there has been more of a focus on self-care than ever before. Perhaps it is because we are understanding more about the value (and pitfalls) of how we live and take care of ourselves. However, a likely contributing factor is the simple fact that many of us *haven't* taken care of ourselves, resulting in burn out, broken relationships, or worse.

A Story from Todd

For years I wore my exhaustion, stress, missed lunches, late nights, and more as a badge of honor. I felt like to be a great leader I had to be everything to everyone, all the time. When I would brag that I hadn't had time for a lunch break in weeks, I never realized what people were internalizing from my "bragging." They began to think, "If he doesn't even take care of himself, how will he ever be able to take care of me and my needs?"

It wasn't until I reached a breaking point where my mind, heart, and body were at their bottom that I stopped to self-reflect. Upon that reflection one of the biggest things I came to

---

understand was I cannot, nor should I, be doing this alone. For a period of time, I began taking anxiety and anti-depression meds and watched my world come into a more clear and healthy focus. Then I began the journey of attending counseling. That's when self-reflection took on a whole new meaning for me. I had a thought partner, disconnected from my daily life, who could help provide clarity and new perspectives.

I always thought if you were going to counseling (or taking medication), that something had to be seriously wrong, or you were falling apart. Boy was I mistaken. I wish someone had made it clear to me far earlier in my life that when we take care of ourselves, we're better for everyone around us. We're able to lead (and be led) in a way that is meaningful. I share this because as you begin your own journey of self-reflection, do not be afraid to seek out supports. To this day I attend therapy once a week and can't even imagine my life without it. Taking care of, and prioritizing, your own mental, physical, and emotional health is a sign of strength, not weakness.

Self-reflection at its core is the intentional willingness to introspectively examine our lives, learning about ourselves in order to help achieve self-awareness. It's reflecting on our thoughts, emotions, and behaviors neutrally and recognizing how they align with our values. It's the ability to take a true look at ourselves and come out on the other side with a comprehensive understanding of our thought processes, needs, and tendencies. Without a willingness to look *inward* first, we will find ourselves focusing on all the wrong things, such as our *outward* circumstances. Pointing the finger. Living as someone who is a victim of our circumstances, rather than responding confidently to them. Responding from a place of perceived lack, rather than from a place of grit and resilience. And ultimately, not realizing that we have what it takes to overcome, prosper, and live and lead at our fullest potential and healthiest selves.

As heavy a paragraph as the one above was, the reality is that so much of who we are is cultivated and germinated in the *power of our thoughts and perspective*. What we focus on, we will empower in our life. Plain and simple. And if we fail to take the time to foster self-reflection in our life, we will be led by our emotions. And we all know the outcome of that story.

> What we focus on, we will empower in our life.

Get Your Mirror Out

Many of our habits, thought patterns, and behaviors are rooted in our subconscious. We find ourselves responding out of places that we don't even realize. Think of it as a type of "control room" that oversees how we think, act, and feel. Yikes. However, if we want to better understand the "why" in a clearer way, we need to place a mirror in front of ourselves to objectively analyze how we are doing, so we can better understand ourselves. This is where self-reflection takes the stage.

Insight from a fellow leader: "*Authentic to me means embracing the things that I enjoy and infusing them in what I do. Drumming at church, Tik Toking at school, or taking a break from the day-to-day operations to sit and read with students in class. When we forget our calling we lose the connection to the ways we can ensure we live in it every day.*"
–Jessica Cabeen, Principal of Alternative Educational Programs

When you self-reflect and become more conscious of what drives you, you can more easily make changes that help you develop and grow yourself into who it is you desire to be—resulting in more impactful leadership, more authentic relationships, and simply more peace. Don't be afraid to speak power into your reflection. Research shows just how powerful speaking our thoughts out loud can be, especially when reflecting. So get in your car, take a drive, and just talk it out....with YOU!

When it comes to self-reflection, it is paramount to understand this does not happen by accident. It takes true intention to quiet our minds and look internally and with honesty about what we feel, what we think, and how we are doing. And it takes commitment to keep pushing through when it's uncomfortable.

A Pen and Paper

One effective way to do this is through journaling. Simply take out a pen and paper and begin writing. No right or wrong. Don't overthink it. Just write. Even if you are feeling a certain way, it's OK. Process through it. But here is the key: *Don't stay there.* Understand that you feel a specific way, but then take a higher perspective. Cultivate gratitude, release forgiveness, or look through a different lens. Make a plan to move *forward*.

When we eliminate the potential for a negative emotion, situation, feeling, or thought to germinate itself in our minds, we then have the opportunity to make a conscious choice in our future. Mahatma Gandhi was famous for saying, "I will not let anyone walk through my mind with their dirty feet." In other words, I will live powerfully so that nothing that steals from my life will have a place in my mind. This is the power of self-reflection and the byproduct of building authenticity.

*"I will not let anyone walk through
my mind with their dirty feet."
-Gandhi*

Keeping a journal is a great way to keep your thoughts together, hold yourself accountable, and create a consistent routine. However, just remember that self-reflection takes time. It is not a thirty second process. It does not need to be hours long, but a 10-15 minute dedicated time of journaling and reflection each day can have a powerful impact on your mind and heart.

Your Quiet Place

The world around us never stops. It never stops demanding, it never stops pulling, and it never stops communicating. It is for this very reason that we must understand the value of solitude—our quiet place. Whether it is a time of prayer, mindfulness, or meditation, the time we spend in this place is fuel for our busy lives. We may not think we need time to reflect, pray, or simply think, but as a result, we may be missing out on the very thing that could be the key to our breakthrough in certain areas.

When it comes to this, there are certain levels in our lives. The first is just as mentioned above. A time in quiet reflection. A time to recalibrate and become keenly aware of how we are doing, what we need, and how we plan to make adjustments for the next leg of our race. This is how we are able to show up big and as our best selves for those around us.

The second layer to this is simply a time of being unplugged. Perhaps it is establishing healthy boundaries (which we will talk about later) where you put your phone down. Or you do not open your computer past 9:00 p.m. Or you do not check emails on Saturdays. Or you go into the woods without your phone (people did survive this for many generations). Whatever this looks like for you, it can be like water for our dry and weary souls. We oftentimes don't realize the toll of the current until we pull ourselves out of the waves and onto the shore for a moment. Learn to disconnect from what pulls on you, so that you can better connect with what is most important to you.

There are many resources that you can find online to help you as you begin to find your disconnected quiet time. Don't be afraid to search Google for videos that help you with breathing exercises (a game-changer) or that guide you in medi-tation as these can be highly beneficial in recalibrating yourself.

> Learn to disconnect from what pulls on you, so that you can better connect with what is most important to you.

Get Introspective to Gain Perspective

Have you ever had a moment by yourself in the car, or listening to a song, or in nature, or on vacation when everything comes into perspective? That instant moment of clarity when you say to yourself, "All of that other stuff doesn't even matter. *This* is all that matters." It's in that moment when we see that our stress, worry, fear, and misplaced focus is oftentimes on the things that don't even matter. When in fact, our family, loved ones, faith, and relationships are the only things that will matter to us when all is said and done. This is the result of a true moment of *introspection*.

When we take an introspective step back, it helps us gain per-spective on what really matters to us. The best way to do this is to ask ourselves really good questions. Recalibrating questions, followed by honest answers. Although there are hundreds of great self-reflection questions to ask yourself, ranging from your relationships to mental/physical health, to your future, some good starter questions are below:

- What am I grateful for?
- Does my morning routine set me up for success?
- What unimportant things are taking my focus off of the import-ant ones?

+ What relationships do I want to improve in my life?
+ What do I know to be true about myself?
+ What are the distractions in my life that I need to remove?
+ What emotions am I avoiding in my life?
+ What do I need to let go of?
+ How do I physically feel? What am I going to do differently?
+ What do I need to prioritize better?
+ What types of people am I surrounding myself with?
+ What am I doing to take care of myself?
+ What are my goals for this next month?

Although these are a drop in the bucket of the many questions to foster self-reflection, two important keys are: **Begin with gratitude and end with vision.** Start off by cultivating appreciation and perspective for all the blessings in your life. It will set your feet on solid ground as you begin reflecting. Then, end by casting vision and setting goals for yourself. It doesn't need to be a five-year plan. It can simply be, "What am I going to do tomorrow? Or in the next fifteen minutes?" Change and success are built in the micro. The small habits. James Clear, author of *Atomic Habits*, poses the question, "If you keep doing what you are about to do today for the next five years, will you end up with more of what you want or less of what you want?" (Clear, 2022).

Closing

Leadership starts from within. Even with the best strategy in the world, *you* ultimately are the difference maker by the way you ensure that you are showing up as your full, best self each day. Remember, it is not a landing point at which you have arrived. It is a *daily* process of renewing your mind, looking inward, being honest with yourself, and having grace for yourself.

When you do these things consistently, you are better equipped internally to infuse life into those around you, love people with patience and empathy, and show up big for those who matter most.

NEXT STEPS:

1. What does your "dashboard" currently look like? Are you feeling out of gas or like you have your "check engine" light on? Or are you fueled up and firing on all cylinders? What steps do you need to take to reflect and recalibrate so that you can live from a healthier place?

2. What value does your quiet place hold in your life? That place you go to pause, breathe, and reflect. How can you ensure you are making time for this on a regular basis? What will that look like?

CHAPTER 4

~

What's at Your Core?

S imply put, your values are your *North Star*. You may also have heard it referred to as your *moral compass*. They are the guiding principles that serve as both guardrails to keep you on course, and catalysts to ensure that you are pursuing what is most important to you. Living our values enables us to make healthy, sound decisions when the heat is turned up, and also builds authenticity as we stay true to them in our relationships and daily life.

Our Early Years

We are deeply shaped by our values and how we live them out. Our life experiences, early life role models, faith, and influential people in our lives have helped craft what these values are. For better or worse. During Tyler's research, he spent time with leaders who reflected back on the early years of their lives and those individuals who helped shape them into the men and women of character and integrity that they are today. They continually went back to the value systems that were modeled for them consistently by those who were influential in their life.

Who are those people in *your* life? Maybe it was a parent, a coach, a mentor, or a faith leader? What did they instill in you? Chances are, it was someone who you were able to see in a number of different contexts, both during successes and challenges. Regardless of *who* it was, your value system has been developing throughout your life journey. These very principles, values, and boundaries are what guides you and grounds you.

A Story from Tyler

Growing up, my dad was a service technician for ATM machines, and would often bring me along on service calls to banks, gas stations, etc. I would perch up in the front seat of his van and enjoy our rides, along with the occasional soda or snack that happened to make its way into the excursion. One Saturday morning, after my dad finished working on an ATM machine at the local Country Fair gas station, we were driving down the road, about ten minutes away.

Suddenly, I saw my dad tip his head back against the headrest and say, "Oh no." Concerned, I leaned myself forward in anticipation of what was to come. Then he said, "I borrowed the cashier's pen to write down something while I was fixing the ATM, and I accidentally took it with me."

Relieved, I said, "It's OK, no problem." To my response, he quickly shared that even with something as insignificant as a pen, the right thing is always the right thing, even if no one will ever know it. As you can guess, we turned around, drove back to the gas station, and returned the cashier's pen, with an apology. A simple act from his value system spoke louder to me than he would ever realize. To this day, nearly thirty years later, this example of integrity resonates in my heart and is a guiding principle for the life I live, the way I lead, and how I strive to raise our own four children.

Conversely, perhaps you came from a background that *didn't* model the greatest values for you—to which I would encourage you to internally reflect and ask yourself: Who do I aspire to be? What attributes and value system do I deep down desire? Who is my ideal, best version of who I dream to be, for myself, my family, and the legacy I want to leave? Because the good news is that your values aren't set in stone. They can change, adapt, and grow. Don't let those difficult periods define who you are and what you believe.

A Story from Todd

Up until my junior high and high school years, I grew up in a home filled with turmoil, struggle, and fear. My mother did her best to set an example of what integrity, grit, and compassion was supposed to look like in the face of pain and abuse.

When I was in 8th grade a man joined our church as the new youth pastor. His name was Troy Sikes. I was immediately drawn to his passion, empathy, the way he spoke to people, and so much more. He showed me what it was like to be a man. The kind of man others wanted to follow. The kind of man who left a legacy without even trying to. In a way he took me under his wing (though I'm pretty sure he made every kid feel that way). Throughout my teenage years, Troy was present during heartbreaks, struggles with faith, my triumphs, my failures, and just plain life. He became the church co-pastor.

He led my (then) fiancée and me through premarital counseling. He is the man who married us. He led my mother's funeral. He dedicated our twins. He's been a light in my life that I don't know where I would be without. He helped me learn and develop my own set of guiding principles. Not only from watching him, but also from having difficult conversations

---

> about who I wanted to be. You see, sometimes those who have a great impact on who we become aren't even family. Yet they sure quickly become like family.

Identifying Your Values

When we identify and live out our values, we will be better able to respond to challenging situations and make decisions with confidence. Additionally, we will find peace in our decisions and purpose in what we say and do. This not only builds authenticity in ourselves, but also builds trust with those around us, as they know we are true to who we say we are, regardless of the circumstance.

When you define your values, you decide what is most important in life. Is it your integrity? Trustworthiness? Honesty? Work-Ethic? Doing your work with excellence? Prioritizing relationships? As you seek to identify your core values, ask yourself this question:

+ What are the values and ideals that define my leadership and who I am as a leader?

Example: Integrity
Value 1:
Value 2:
Value 3:

Next, once you have established your top 3-5 values, write down the actual definition of your values, as it relates to you and your life.

Example: Integrity	Value Definition: *Always doing the right thing, even if it's the hard thing.*
Value 1:	Value Definition:
Value 2:	Value Definition:
Value 3:	Value Definition:

As you identify the values that are most integral to who you are, take a moment and reflect:

+ Imagine your time on this earth has come to a close. As your loved ones share out at your funeral about who you were as a person, what will they say? Does this align with the values that you have identified as most important to you? If not, what adjustments need to be made, so that you live, lead, and love those around you in a way that is true to who you are and desire to become. That isn't only who you are but also how others take you in. That is the process of building authenticity.

> What do I want people to say about my life and who I was as a person, leader, spouse, parent, friend, etc.?

Your Values Put to the Test

Leaders who are guided by their values are vital in today's world. Authentic leaders are people who keep core values in their crosshairs at all times. Those values serve as the lenses through which they view every situation and circumstance. In fact, Fred Walumbwa, a seminal voice in

Authentic Leadership Theory, emphasized that when you internalize your morals and values, they become the standard for measuring all of your actions and behaviors, regardless of the situation, people involved, or external pressure from society, culture, individuals, etc. (Walumbwa et al.,2008).

Leading authentically and being true to yourself means to live out your values—regardless of the pressure to conform or compromise. Regardless of how you will be treated or judged. And to take it a step further, when you as a leader develop your values and principles *before* you find yourself in a crisis, you are better prepared to keep your

> When authentic leaders are grounded in their values, they become the standard for measuring all of their actions and behaviors.

bearings during difficult decisions and dilemmas. You are able to make more sound decisions. As a result, you need not battle internally with the right choice when your authenticity is challenged, because you are steadfast in your principles. Through this, you will find peace in your adversity and also in the decisions that you make.

It is relatively easy to be true to your values when things are going well—but when they are challenged, are you steadfast to who you are? This is the foundation of authenticity. Courageously being true to yourself and your most deeply held values and morals. As the saying goes, "A calm sea never made a skilled sailor." If we never have opposition or obstacles in our lives that require us to lean on our values, we miss out on the great opportunity to develop the internal fortitude and capacity to stand firm when it matters most. Don't view those challenges as a negative thing. Instead view challenges as opportunities for *growth*.

As a matter of fact, during Tyler's research on interviewing leaders and their authentic leadership development, there were times when leaders were at a crossroads and their values were put to the test—and they were actually willing to resign from their position before they compromised who they were. Now *that* is authenticity.

> **Insight from a fellow leader:** *"I set boundaries and I stick to them. It is OK to say "No" and to prioritize. I communicate how I feel with people, and I don't hold it in. I take time for myself, and I do not feel guilty about it."*
> —Cicely Lewis, School Librarian and Author

Values Attract Values

There is no one "right" set of values. However, when you establish them, you will be better poised to lead from them, and attract others with similar value systems. As a matter of fact, research has shown that authentic leadership is positively related to employees personally identifying with their leader and similar values (Avolio et al., 2004).

When people find a reflection of their own values in their leader, it emboldens them to ground themselves in those personal values. It creates a value-driven culture. It creates a common undercurrent. Meaning, your values and moral compass actually attract like-minded people of character, integrity, and authenticity who will add value to your organization far beyond the bottom line. Keep in mind these are not "yes men," but people who share a similar value system and integrity.

We will talk more about this later, but it is important to know that people don't simply just see what you do. They see *who you are.* And who you are matters.

> It is important to know that people don't simply just see what you do. They see who you are. And who you are matters.

39

Your Values in Action

Living our values on a daily basis is most certainly a journey, rather than a destination. As we pursue and build authenticity in our lives, we are continually "moving the needle" toward the person we desire to be. That is why our values must not only be at the forefront of our minds, but evident in our choices, behaviors, and examples we set for those around us.

An example of this was evident in a leader we spoke with regarding his value system and principles he leads by. One of his core values is, "never cut corners in life," and lives daily by the saying that his dad instilled in him at a young age of, "hard work, done well, feels good." His value system informs his actions, and as a result navigates him through life. It is the standard by which he lives, leads, and models for those around him. This *daily walk* as a leader is where the rubber meets the road. Picture yourself in your organization. In your home. When no one is watching. When there is no one to gain from or no one to impress. Who are you? This defines you as a person. Leaders have to walk their talk and demonstrate their commitment to their values.

There is too much at stake for you to be pulled off course, but as leaders it is inevitable that our authenticity will be challenged and that we will make mistakes. Perhaps the fear of failure will knock at your door. Maybe it will be the pressure to conform based on societal or cultural norms or opinions. Perhaps it will come from the pressure from others in leadership or stakeholders for you to make a decision in contrast to your value system. In those moments, your authenticity is put to the test.

In Bill George's Book, *Discover Your True North*, he interviewed Narayana Murthy, the founder and CEO of Infosys. She said, "*Leaders with principles are less likely to get bullied or pushed around because they can draw clear lines in the sand… the softest pillow is a clear conscience*" (George, 2015, p. 108).

Before you leave this chapter, identify your values. Put pen to paper. Reflect on them regularly, and self-assess honestly. Just as importantly, communicate your values to those around you so they can help keep you accountable. Don't keep them to yourself. Your value-system should be known and articulated to those you love and lead, so that they can know what to expect from you, even when the going gets tough. Let them encourage you when you need to make the *right decision*, even when it's the *hard one*.

NEXT STEPS:

1. You spent time identifying and listing your personal values throughout the chapter. Reflect back on them. How will you be intentional to keep those on the forefront of your decision making and how you live your life?

2. Think back to your own upbringing. Who impacted you in a positive way? In what ways could you reach out to them today to let them know how that affected you?

CHAPTER 5

Who Has Your Back?

A Story from Tyler

I'll never forget the time I sat and talked to a friend, who in his 30's, began taking steps towards creating the life they truly desired. He began to capture vision, prioritize relationships, and leaned into the process of identifying who he wanted to become for his family and his future. He was a dad of young kids, and began realizing the responsibility he had to live and lead his family with vision, integrity, and excellence. It was a defining season in his life.

As we sat and talked, he shared with me one of his most impactful reflections: "I wish I would have opened up and let people into my life over the years," he said. "All this time, I struggled to find purpose and tried to do things on my own, which landed me right back in the same place I was before. There were people in my life that cared about me, but I simply didn't invite them in and listen. I would love to go back and do these last 10 years over again."

Sometimes in life, we find ourselves feeling stuck. As a result, we feel the need to work through those things alone–whether out of embarrassment, the fear of appearing inadequate, or even believing the lie that the people closest to us will look at us differently. We build up walls, board up windows, and make others believe we've got it all under control.

But the truth is, life is not meant to be lived alone. We need the people in our lives who we trust to speak truth to us, support us on our journey, and use their relational access point to speak into our lives about our "blind spots" that are stealing from us. However, this all starts with a humble invitation to welcome feedback into our life–even when it's not always what we want to hear. Because that's when we need to hear it the most.

Your Support Team

There is such value in a personal community in a leader's life. Not solely for encouragement, but for support and accountability. Reflect for a moment on those people in your circle who you deeply trust to speak into your life. Maybe it's your spouse, your best friend, a coworker, your pastor, or a mentor. Generally, this is not a large group of people, but an inner circle who knows you deeply and who are the ones that are there for you, through thick or thin.

Do you give those people permission to share with you when they see you fading off course? More importantly, when they do, are you open to their feedback? Or do you lash out with excuses and embarrassment? One of the greatest catalysts to personal growth is our willingness to pull the veil back and welcome the feedback of others. Your support team members are the people who have faith in you and love you for who you are. But they care about you too much to let things rob you of your potential. They are not solely concerned about your personal successes, but first and foremost care about *you* as a person. Those people in our lives are a gift. They are also few and far between.

Perhaps you are overcommitting in an area and leaving another facet of your life to suffer as a result. Maybe when addressing certain topics or people you are not hitting the mark with your approach or intentions. Or perhaps you are simply wearing yourself out to the point that you are not bringing your best self to the most important things in your life. Your support team knows your heart and has your best interests in mind. They are the ones who are willing to say, "I see this area in your life that is holding you back from who you are intending to be. Would you be willing to take some time to reflect in this area?" And they do this from a place of love. That's what makes their feedback so incredibly powerful.

> **Insight from a fellow leader:** "Working to be an authentic leader means having a close circle, my "peloton" of mentors, friends, family, and peers to give me feedback and share honest reflections, dialogue, and thought partnering around. They help keep my moral, ethical, and professional compass alive and in check."
> —Alice Lee, Director of Secondary Education

Your support team can provide affirmation, advice, suggestions, perspective, and most importantly, love. Many times as leaders, we are judged by our output and find external validation in what we accomplish. But your support system—your inner circle—loves you all the same. What they care about is *you*, and it is important to recognize that your vulnerability to open up with them and embrace their feedback is meant for your *growth*, not your harm.

Bill George shared that in challenging times, leaders need a solid network of trusted relationships with people available to council and

Feedback is a gift.

care for them. This can provide leaders with confidence to listen to their inner voice, even when outsiders are attacking or criticizing their decisions. A support team can provide resilience to get through the hard times and to recognize what is truly important in life (George, 2015).

Sometimes, we simply need people to be a sounding board and listen. Perhaps it's a gentle reminder to prioritize what matters most, which serves as a guide to stay true to your course and not let the pressures, responsibilities, or even critics in your life shift you away from where you are going.

> **Insight from a fellow leader:** *"This is hard work. Your mindset needs to be right and unwavering in all you do. You need to surround yourself with people who will grow you and challenge you as well, so you grow and share your core values."*
> –Buckley Cook, Curriculum Director

Bill Johnson, pastor of Bethel Church in Redding, CA once said, "If you don't live by the praises of men, you won't die by their criticism" (Johnson, 2011). There will always be those in your life that critique, judge, and make assumptions about you. That will never change or disappear. But it is your support system and tribe that are there to remind you of who you are and challenge you in the areas that are holding you back. To be your anchor.

> We need people in our lives who we trust to give us honest feedback.

The Value of Accountability

In many aspects, the word "accountability" has a negative connotation. However, accountability can be one of the most powerful tools in your life. In your relationships with your support team whom you trust, accountability might look like confiding in them regarding an area of struggle. Maybe it's an issue of self-discipline with scheduling priorities, or focusing on growing in some of your soft skills, or even a private situation. This takes tremendous vulnerability, but there is power in shining a light on the area and committing to growth with the support of people who believe in you. There is always immense strength in vulnerability.

In a different light, accountability need not be related to an area in which you are struggling. It can be centered around a goal or focal point that you are targeting in your life. Either way, when we invite people into our journey and are honest with what we do and do not want in our lives, those trusted individuals can remind us of where our guardrails are while also serving as our greatest encouragers.

360 Degree Feedback

Because you want to live and lead with authenticity and impact, leaning into feedback is essential. However, it can be uncomfortable at times. It doesn't always feel great to sense that someone is putting your shortcomings on display, so remember that it is a matter of *perspective*. Think of the relief you feel when a friend quietly saves you from the pepper or lettuce in your teeth. They are looking out for you because they *have your back*. They want what's best for you.

Opening yourself up to feedback can be a fairly humbling experience. Many times, we assume that if we say to someone, "If there is anything you see in my life, I want you to let me know," that the response will be, "Well, now that you asked, let me get out my laundry list of shortcomings that everyone sees, besides you."

That alone can be enough to shy people away from opening up to feedback. However, remember that your support team has your best interests in mind. They see the good in you. They are cheering you on and want you to live as the very best you. True supporters in your life are the ones that celebrate your wins, and are genuinely overjoyed when you succeed. Find those people and don't let them go.

Also keep in mind that some people in your life will bring their opinions and advice whether you asked for it or not. And it won't always be coming from a place of love. Those people should be taken with a grain of salt because they are not part of your true inner circle.

When it comes to welcoming feedback in your life, it starts with the humility to *ask*. Because this is such a rarity in life—for someone to humble themselves and say, "I don't want anything to hold me back. Speak into my life," it will take an invitation from you to that person or two whom you trust. Don't just assume people will tell you. Be willing to ask them questions. One powerful question to ask others is, "How do you experience me when…" This eliminates closed questioning that would otherwise elicit a yes or no response from them.

Additionally, being specific in the areas you desire feedback in is helpful to those individuals who are supporting you. Maybe it is regarding our demeanor in a meeting, or how we engage in social settings. Perhaps it is regarding relational dynamics. What if it was a simple aspect like your body language that regularly communicated a different message than you were intending when you were talking to others? You would want to know!

Finally, and possibly the most pivotal aspect of welcoming feedback from others, is how you respond when they provide it to you. Honest evaluation can be a vulnerable thing that can stir up feelings of self-consciousness or even defensiveness—especially if we feel misrepresented from our true intentions in a situation. That can easily lead to excuses and hurt feelings. However, we want to create an open, receptive conduit between ourselves and the people we trust. It's hard, but always worth it. If we bite back every time someone shares feedback with us, or if our first response is always to rationalize, defend, or blame others, they will simply stop telling us. You may not always agree, but with an open mind and honest follow-up reflection and self-assessment, there might just be some truth for you to apply to your life and adjust your sails. Remember, feedback is a gift.

At its core, leaning into feedback about your blind spots is essential for you as a leader, because your growth directly impacts those you lead. And they're called blind spots for a reason. If we don't allow others to help us grow, we miss out on important learning moments. Just the same, the lid on your growth and potential *also* impacts those you lead.

> **Feedback is essential in your life because your growth directly impacts those you lead.**

The Johari Window

Have you ever had the blood pressure spiking experience of driving down the interstate and as you try to transition lanes you hear the blare of a car horn? As you quickly swerve back into your original lane, you realize they were in your blind spot. Think of that inner circle that we discussed as your mirrors, which can help give you the vital information necessary to keep you in the right lane, going the right direction. These blind spots can affect virtually every area of our life—our relationships, our performance, and, ultimately, our impact on the things that are most important to us. They can become the source of habits and patterns that many times leave us stuck, whether we realize it or not. And as a result, we can't move forward or grow in an area that we don't even know exists.

Below is a graphic called the "Johari Window." It was developed in the 1950's by psychologists Joseph Luft and Harrington Ingram as a basic tool to represent the collective value of our individual experiences, views, attitudes, skills, thoughts, intentions, and emotions. The benefit to becoming aware of these areas of our life is that a more well-rounded understanding of our personal strengths and weaknesses can provide us with the information we need to better navigate our relationships with others and understand our own self (Luft & Ingram, 1955).

The premise behind the window is to serve as a map for the purpose of identifying and improving important components of our life, such as:

+ Self-Awareness
+ Personal Development
+ Communication
+ Interpersonal relationships

The chart is made up of four quadrants. Together, they are meant to contribute to forming a complete awareness of ourselves:

THE JOHARI WINDOW

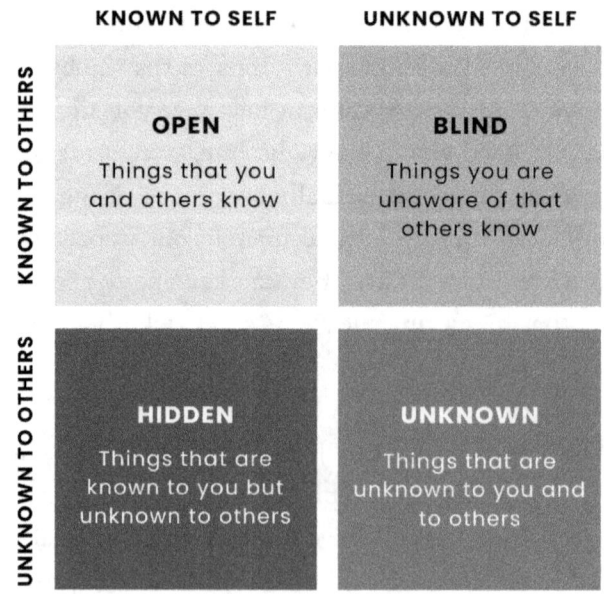

1. Open Area

The first area, known as the "open area," represents information that you and others both know about you. This information can be anything about you, including emotions, behaviors, skills, feelings, opinions. Oftentimes, the bigger this area is, the greater opportunity there is to develop trusted, authentic, and transparent relationships with others.

As a result, your open area will be larger for those who you know well, specifically your support team. Conversely, your open area will naturally be smaller with those whom you have less depth of relationship with. It is important to note, however, that the goal is not to transition *everything* into the open area for all people. There is a tactful balance as leaders with private or confidential information about ourselves. It is important to find the appropriate balance to ensure we are opening ourselves up to those who matter most and those who we have invited to speak truth and honest feedback to us.

2. Blind Area

The second area, known as the "blind area," represents all the things that you are not aware of about yourself. However, others around you are aware of these traits or behaviors. By receiving information or feedback from others, individuals can gain insight about themselves and improve. Our blind spots don't only pertain to the "negative" aspects of our lives, however. We can also have positive traits or behaviors that we are not aware of. It is important that we know those things as well! All of it matters.

This blind spot region mostly contains ways to develop our personal growth. By welcoming people to speak to these blind spots, we can make better-informed decisions regarding our behaviors, responses, and approaches to situations. It is in this quadrant that we can use constructive criticism and feedback to move the needle towards becoming a more effective leader, colleague, spouse, or friend. Finally, as we grow through information in the blind spot area, we in turn expand our open area as well.

3. Hidden Area

The third area in the Johari window model is known as the "hidden area." This section represents things that are known to you, but not to others around you. It may consist of private information, emotions, or experiences you do not wish to reveal about yourself to others. If an individual trusts another person, they may wish to reveal something personal about themselves. This is how strong and deeper relationships are built.

4. Unknown Area

Finally, the fourth area, known as the "unknown area," represents the unknown places where no communication exists. Neither the individual nor those around them are aware of it. The unknown area may contain information such as subconscious memories from childhood, hidden beliefs, or feelings the individual is unaware of.

Although this model is simply a visual tool to foster self-awareness, it can be a benefit to improving relationships, communication, and more. When we gain a better understanding of our personal strengths and weaknesses by taking into account the views from other people, it can be a catalyst to both our personal and professional development.

> **Insight from a fellow leader:** "I am a self-aware person by nature who understands that no one is perfect and there is always room for improvement. I strive to always be open to feedback, constructive criticism, and often request it from those around me in the name of personal growth. As people, we need to be open to the idea that we can always improve, and growth is always good. If Michael Jordan stayed

late in the gym to continue practicing free throws to get better, then we
can all continue putting in the extra work to get better, too.
-James Appleton, Business Owner and Podcaster

Balanced Processing in Leadership

The final area to highlight in this chapter is the term "balanced process-ing," which is one of the four core components of Authentic Leader-ship. This term represents a leader's ability to objectively evaluate and understand both the positive and negative aspects of themselves and their situations.

Kernis (2003) referred to this component of authenticity as the ability to avoid ignoring, exaggerating, or distorting one's knowledge and experiences. Further, he noted that balanced processing demands that leaders avoid rationalizing their weaknesses and requires them to include even their lesser qualities, attributes, and emotions in consid-eration of their self-assessment, which in turn helps avoid ego defense mechanisms.

In other words, authentic leaders can more objectively process infor-mation because there is less concern with being right, how they look, and ultimately, less ego involvement. As a result, they can be more aware of their emotions, the lenses through which they are viewing situations, and areas in which they may not be optimally performing or living as their best self. Additionally, authentic leaders have the ability to balance their extrinsic and intrinsic motivations. It is so important that as leaders we understand what drives us in order to maintain a healthy decision-mak-ing perspective. Some leaders find success, recognition, and stature based on their accomplishments, but authentic leaders derive a sense of mean-ing and purpose in life from their intrinsic motivations.

Finally, Illies et al. (2005) suggested that balanced processing is at the heart of personal integrity and character. Through the balanced processing of authentic leaders and openness to learning and different perspectives, individuals can better establish and deepen authentic relationships with others. As a result, this leads to mutual respect, openness, and trust.

Closing

Your support team in life is truly a gift. They are not simply there to slap your hand when you are off course, but they are there to encourage you, believe in you, and remind you of who you are when things get tough. They are your anchor. They are there to listen, as well as provide feedback. Don't discount the value of these people. If you are feeling vulnerable asking, that's OK. It takes courage to say, "Will you speak into my life?" But you will be a better husband, wife, father, mother, and leader because of it.

If you're struggling identifying who these people are in your life, reflect on people who you have around you that you respect and ask them to speak into you. Take a moment and reflect on these simple questions below. Let no day go to waste as you pursue becoming your most authentic and impactful self!

NEXT STEPS:

1. Who are the 2 or 3 most trusted individuals in your life (your support team) that you could turn to if you needed help/advice?

2. Do these individuals have permission to speak into your life? Do you invite them to provide you *honest* feedback?

3. Find time this week to ask someone in your circle for honest feedback about an area in your life and write down their response. Spend time reflecting (not deflecting) the feedback and list an actionable way for you to grow.

CHAPTER 6

~

It's Not Just about You

Ask yourself this question and reflect for a moment:

What would your team or organization look like if everyone was just like you?

- What would the culture look like?
- What would the value system of your team be?
- Are relationships built on trust, honesty, and integrity?
- How would your team respond to challenges or adversity?
- Are people challenged to grow and develop into their fullest potential?

This humbling and powerful overarching question of self-reflection is a fantastic plumbline for us as leaders to regularly look inwards and identify if we are, in fact, living out who we say we are, and, in turn, creating an ecosystem in which the people we lead can also live up to their fullest potential. Because at the end of the day, we aren't just leading programs. We aren't simply managing goals and deadlines. We aren't just checking things off a to-do list. We are leading *people*, and we have the unique access point as leaders to speak into their lives and become a catalyst for their authentic growth as well.

As leaders, we have the privilege to develop people from where they are to where they can be. But that doesn't happen by accident. It takes daily intention and commitment to *grow ourselves* as people and leaders, so that we can bring our best to those we serve. It takes work. Because our growth is far more than simply for ourselves.

Untapped

We have amazing people on our teams and in our organizations. High potential people. And by high potential people, we don't just mean "high performers." There is a difference. These are high *potential* people with tremendous ability beyond what they even realize that many times go untapped on our teams. And that's the most exciting part. The unrealized potential that you can help unlock.

Authentic leadership goes beyond just ensuring that *we* are living healthy so that we can lead healthy, integrated, balanced, and value-driven lives. Authentic leadership is also about committing to the greatness inside of those around us. Authentic leaders are willing to see beyond the "stuff" that our people may have, and lock in like a heat-seeking missile onto the gold that is within them. Unfortunately, many times people don't even realize it's there.

Perhaps they have settled into their roles in life and at work. Perhaps they have been discouraged by others as to their ability or potential to make a difference. Perhaps they battle with limiting beliefs, self-doubt, or even fears. Or perhaps they've never been allowed the chance to shine. Whatever it may

> Our greatest calling as leaders is to grow and develop people into their fullest potential.

be, as leaders we have the incredible privilege to speak into their life, shine a spotlight on who they really are, and most importantly, create an environment that will challenge them and foster their growth.

If Not You, Then Who?

A Story from Tyler

Think back for a moment to a time in your life when someone believed in you. Someone who not only inspired you, but also truly saw something in you and called it out of you. Someone who encouraged you when you didn't have courage. Someone who empowered you when you simply weren't sure of yourself.

For me, it was Mrs. Freeburg, my 11th grade anatomy teacher. She was so full of love, and was one of those teachers who ended up being equal parts "mom" and equal parts "teacher" for most of the kids. However, because of the way she cared about you and always saw the best in you, there was a weight on her words when she spoke to you. No matter the student, she never gave up, and they knew it.

I remember being a 16-year-old kid (and acting like one). Nothing over the top, but certainly not performing to my potential. One day, she asked me to stay after class. As I held back after the bell rang, I was expecting to get reprimanded for my behavior. Instead, it was quite the contrary. Sitting on the edge of a desk, Mrs. Freeburg sat silent for a moment, eyes to the floor. She then looked up with tears in her eyes, and said, "Tyler, you are so much better than this. Your future is so bright. Don't get caught up in anything that would distract you from who you really are."

Speechless and without even realizing it, tears filled my eyes as well. She took the time to see the potential inside me and loved me enough to remind me, even when I wasn't putting my best on display.

That morning after Anatomy class was a defining moment in my life. She literally helped shape what I saw in myself and who I was capable of becoming. It was because of Mrs. Freeburg that I became a teacher, and it is with her same heart for calling out the gold in others that I aim to lead with.

As the principal of an elementary school, one of Todd's favorite things was helping his team see the greatness in themselves that he saw in them. As you get to know, truly know, those around you, you begin to see immense possibilities. As leaders, it's our responsibility to push them and grow them into their best selves. I (Todd) always loved asking them to join a team, or try something new, or attend/lead a different kind of professional development, and watch as the doubt crept in, and they weren't quite sure they had the correct skillset. But the truly exciting part was watching them take the leap, because they trusted me, and see them walk into their brilliance.

Truett Cathy, founder of Chick Fil-A once said, "How do you know if a man or woman needs encouragement? They are breathing" (Cathy, 2015). This simple yet profound idea of living as an encourager applies far beyond giving someone a pat on the back and telling them they have what it takes. Authentic leaders understand the value of literally seeing who people really are, and calling it out of them. It means believing in them when they don't even believe in themselves!

As a leader, you might be the only person in someone's life who has the opportunity to develop the gifts, abilities, and potential inside them. Sure, there are influential people who have come and gone throughout their life, such as their parents, a mentor, their spouse, a pastor, etc., but why not you? Challenge yourself to reframe your thinking as having the ability to be the one in their life to say, "Set your eyes on a higher perspective. Here is what I see inside you. This is who you really are. Now, let's go!"

A Story from Tyler

Years ago, I was working with a staff member who had tremendous potential. She was an idea factory, truly loved the people she served, and, most importantly, possessed a teachable heart. However, through years of life experiences, self-doubt, and challenging seasons of life, she simply did not believe in herself. She was her own harshest critic, and downplayed the potential and impact that she could have in our school, on her students, and on those around her. She didn't feel that people wanted to hear what she said, and lived with a lid on who she really was.

After a few years of building our relationship, speaking to her potential, and creating opportunities for self-reflection and personal growth, she did what most aren't willing to do. She began doing the challenging, uncomfortable, and time-consuming work on the *inside*. She realized that it wasn't *what she did* that defined her worth and identity, but rather it was *who she is* that defined it.

Never in my professional life have I seen someone lean into that uncomfortable and humbling process of personal growth like she did. She was open, teachable, and willing to embrace feedback. She renewed her mind to no longer be defined by her own limiting beliefs, but rather who she *desired to become*. And as a result, she has grown and become a resounding voice in our school, our district, and beyond. Would she say it was a walk in the park? No. But that is what authenticity looks like, and it is always worth it.

The call of leadership is one of utmost importance. It can feel challenging and many times arduous when it comes to working with people who already have their mind made up about *who* they are and *how* things are. But that is no way to live. And just as you are in pursuit of growing yourself as an authentic leader, you can help move the needle in the lives around you to do the same. It's incredibly fulfilling work.

Gold Digging

Danny Silk, founder of *Loving on Purpose*, loves to refer to developing the *gold* inside of people (Silk, 2009), and it is the perfect visual for our responsibility as leaders. However, we can all agree that people can be messy at times.

Close your eyes for a second and think about the people you lead. The people in your life. What is your first response? Do you look upon them fondly? Do you feel stressed because of the pull and strain on you? Like there is a constant demand, like you are the parent? Or, as much as you don't want to, do you feel the need to micromanage or keep certain people at arm's length?

If you feel these ways, we want to validate those feelings and tell you that is OK. Having that awareness is a really important thing. However, today we are challenging you to lean into those feelings. Because there will always be people like that no matter where you lead. But at the end of the day, you are responsible for **your** heart towards them.

> Every person you lead has gold inside of them.

Being a leader who leads from the inside-out does so by rolling up your sleeves and loving your people, even in their mess. Even when they bring their worst—because they inevitably will at times. But you have the opportunity to see the greatness inside of them. To see the gold.

Some people have gold inside them so evident that you can practically trip over it. It's right there, shining, easy for everyone to see. But for others, you need to dig a little bit. Scrub it clean. Get some dirt under your fingernails. But the extra effort is totally worth it. Because they are always worth it.

> **Insight from a fellow leader:** *"Empowering others by recognizing strengths has been the most successful approach to bringing out the best in those around me. Once those strengths are identified, providing crafted or natural opportunities for them to shine allows the individual to build confidence and experience in that skill. Ultimately, allowing others to be their best increases the output of an entire organization."*
> –Adam Dovico, Administrator, Speaker, Author

A Culture of Honor

So, what does it look like to love and lead every person on your team with authenticity? No matter the team you lead, there will always be a spectrum of people–those you support and are supportive of you and those you are… you get the point. While it's easy to invest in and love those who believe in your vision and make significant contributions to your team, how do we authentically lead those who are more challenging?

As you might have guessed, it all starts *within*. It begins with the posture of your heart towards that person, based on who they are, not their shortcomings. It's about understanding that most people genuinely try to bring their best in life, but are simply wounded through life experiences, hurts, and relationships. People generally don't purposefully try to be jaded, and don't find joy in tension. They oftentimes are trapped in self-preservation, fear, or unprocessed pain that creates cynicism or puts up walls to connection and relationships.

Bill Johnson, Pastor of Bethel Church in Redding, CA so perfectly depicts what creating a culture of honoring others looks like in our organizations. He said, "A culture of honor is celebrating who a person is without stumbling over who they are not" (Silk, 2009, p. 25). What a powerful reminder as a leader in all aspects of our life!

Think about a challenging child in a 3rd grade classroom. One that you know has a tough home life, lacks support, and even struggles to have basic needs met. As a result, they act out, struggle to focus, and can even be combative. Now, think about the sacrifices we as adults make for students like that. Those are the kids we skip our lunch to spend time with. Those are the kids we stay after school with to help catch up on work. Those are the students we go to Walmart for in the evenings to buy a new pair of winter boots because their old ones are worn out. We will do anything for those challenging students, because we know the cards they have been dealt and the unseen struggles they face. We want to be a champion for that child.

Fast forward thirty years. Perhaps those challenging people in our organizations and teams are those same children, just bigger and older? Ones that have had tough cards dealt to them, ones that have dealt with being let down, and ones that are impacted by their life experiences? Ones that sometimes can act like that third-grade child, because life has had them create coping mechanisms that haven't aged well? As leaders, it can be easy to count those people out, because they are difficult. Now, we understand that you won't always be able to change their behaviors, their attitudes, or their perspectives. What you can change, however, is *yours*.

> **Authentic leaders love their people, even in their mess.**

Authentic leaders love their people, even in their mess. They understand that no matter who it is, they deserve the best of them. What if you spent time investing relationally in your most challenging people? What if you began calling out the "gold" inside of them instead of focusing on the dirt? You might be surprised. But regardless of the outcome, *you* are in charge of your heart towards them. That is authenticity.

Examine Your Toolbox

Simon Sinek said, "Great leaders don't blame the tools they are given. They work to sharpen them" (Sinek, 2019). Think about your team and the environment you have created. Do you foster a culture in which people are propelled towards their potential? Or do they remain "dull" under your leadership? Deep down, everyone desires to belong and to be a part of something great. It is intrinsically wired in all of us. Unfortunately, when people have limiting beliefs about themselves that they are not good enough or don't belong, it can become a self-fulfilling prophecy in their lives, which leads to their disconnect. However, as their leader, *you* might be the best chance for them to ever reach their potential. By communicating the value and importance of who they are, not simply what they do for your team, it could be a difference maker in how they view themselves.

Have you ever been around someone who, just by being in their presence made you want to stand up a little taller and straighter? When you are around them, you simply want to "up your game" and be a better version of yourself? There are some attributes and characteristics about these people that you desire to see in yourself, and it inspires you to want to pursue it. We have the ability to instill that feeling in every person we lead—at home, in our families, and in our friendships. Take a moment and reflect: When people are around us, do they leave wanting to become better? Remember,

> Deep down, everyone desires to belong and to be a part of something great.

it is not just what you say that makes an impact; rather, it is who you are that speaks volumes.

The Paradox of Personal Growth

You are most likely on this journey to build authenticity in your life because you understand the value and calling you have to impact the world around you. Your love for those in your life, coupled with that intrinsic flame to live at your fullest potential makes sacrifice worth it, and gives purpose to the growing pains. That being said, the paradox at the heart of personal growth is that we don't grow and become our best selves when that is simply our *only* goal. Being focused on ourselves never brings out the best in us. Rather, we grow and become authentic, noble, open-hearted, and impactful when we live for something *greater* than ourselves—such as our faith or serving the potential in those around us.

In a culture where much of our focus is on our input—what we can get out of life, what we can obtain, what we can accomplish, etc.—authentic leaders understand that uncomfortable inner work must be done so that their *output* truly makes a difference and impacts the lives of those around them. This even means loving and pouring into those who are difficult or don't understand the value that you bring to the organization. Authentic leaders do it anyway. Because they understand that in order to grow fully, it comes with *loving and serving fully*.

Your Life On Display

You may have heard the saying, "If your actions inspire others to dream more, learn more, do more, and become more, you are a leader." These words ring true for every aspect of our lives. Whether it is in your family, your marriage, your friendships, or your work, your life is your story on display. If *you* were the one watching it, would *you* be inspired?

People do not expect you to be perfect (at least most of them). But they do expect you to be *real*. Too often we can get caught in the trap of perfectionism as leaders, which ultimately leads to stress and even paralysis of growth because we are afraid to take risks. In reality, the people you lead value honesty, transparency, ownership, and vulnerability. These four words can be unnerving for someone who is not grounded in who they really are. However, for an authentic leader, these four words are pillars of strength and identity.

The Trust Factor

Have you ever been around someone so "real" that it is refreshing? You never have to question "which one of them" you are going to get. They could be having their best day or worst day, yet they are true and steadfast to who they are. People like this are good for the soul, because they limit anxiety and fear in those they lead and have relationships with.

Of all of the important qualities of a leader, the case can be made that being trustworthy is near the top. Just like in any meaningful relationship in life, when there is trust, it unlocks another layer of your connection and exponentially expands the possibilities and potential of that relationship. As we all know, trust isn't built in a day, and it doesn't happen by chance. It can't be "implemented," and it can't be forced. It is the byproduct of authentic, vulnerable, transparent relationships that over time establish equity and result in strong teams and powerful cultures—whether at home or work. Trust can be lost quickly, but through hard work and a sincere desire, trust can also be gained back.

Throughout the first few chapters of this book, we discussed the importance of leading from our values, fostering self-awareness, and living transparently. As much as these attributes and life processes grow who we are as leaders, they play a paramount role in developing trust, culture, and collective efficacy in our teams as well.

Research by Gardner et al. (2005) on the development of authentic leaders found that as people observe their leader displaying an understanding of self-awareness and engaging in transparent decision-making that reflects integrity and values, they develop trust in their leader that actually fosters open and authentic behaviors in the employees as well. Furthermore, over time this translates into developing a value-driven culture that is grounded in those characteristics of transparency, trust, and integrity. In other words, the trust you build becomes the conduit to actually helping develop authenticity in those you lead.

Vulnerability = Strength

That's right, there is that "vulnerability" word again. Some of you may be reading that word and cringing, as you have walked the lonely, winding road of leadership that has been marred by betrayal, criticism, or judgment. As a result, the idea of being "vulnerable" with those you lead may feel like tossing yourself to the wolves or surrendering any amount of authority you feel you have left. It can be downright terrifying and debilitating. However, in a paradigm-shifting concept, we believe that vulnerability may be the very lifeline you need to reconnect with those you lead and find grace for yourself as a leader.

You are likely familiar with Brené Brown, a professor and sociologist who has written several books about why vulnerability is an integral part of success, both in a personal and an organizational context. She defines vulnerability as "uncertainty, risk, and emotional exposure" (Brown, 2012, p. 2). This doesn't mean shooting from the hip on tough decisions and sharing intimate details of your personal life. Rather, it is a call to show up to work and life in an honest way where the "real" you and your values shine through, no matter the circumstances.

What does this look like? Simple (albeit uncomfortable) acts such as admitting when you're wrong or owning up to the fact that you do not have all the answers. This builds trust. This is the human side of leadership that people connect with, rally around, and desire.

We tend to adopt a default position towards self-preservation as we move through our lives. However, being transparent and vulnerable as a leader is not a sign of weakness. It's a compelling and powerful way to build trust with those you lead, and modeling vulnerability increases the likelihood that others will become more transparent as well. Your vulnerability lays the foundation for the culture you want to build. Because whether you like it or not, all of you shows up in every part of your life. You can't leave pieces of you in the car or at the door.

NEXT STEPS:

1. How do you find yourself loving those you lead, even when things get messy? What mistakes have you made in the past? How can you lead differently in the future?

2. In what ways can you develop the skill of being more vulnerable and real, even when it feels uncomfortable?

CHAPTER 7

Your Team, Your Culture, Your Opportunity

Stephen R. Covey said, "Leadership is communicating to people their worth and potential so clearly that they come to see it in themselves" (Covey, 2013). This is such a great depiction of our role as authentic leaders. Throughout this book we have explored many of the core components of the development of authentic leadership, along with the tremendous responsibility we have to invest in every person we lead, no matter how challenging. So, what does this look like in a practical sense? How do we genuinely invest in those we lead while still moving forward the vision of our organizations that we serve?

The Team We Build

We are only as good as the teams that we build. If we are too concerned with keeping our arms wrapped around everything in fear of what might happen if we let go, we miss out on the opportunity to tap into the amazing people who are on our teams. As a result, we lose out on the exponential power of empowerment.

A Story from Tyler

Most of us are in the leadership roles that we are in because someone believed in us. Someone most likely saw our potential and was a catalyst for helping us navigate through life and into roles that maximized our impact and helped fulfill our vision for our life. I suspect with a moment of reflection, that person or people will come to mind.

For me, it was Dr. Stephanie Williams. She was a mentor early in my career, and instrumental in where I am today. Because I desired to become a principal, she joined me in the pursuit. She aligned herself alongside me and said, "OK, what do we need to do to get you there?"

During the workday, she gave up her lunch time to sit with me and let me in on her day. She provided me opportunities to lead and engage in experiences that I would have never had otherwise. She nudged me outside my comfort zone and communicated confidence in what I was attempting to learn. But most importantly, she continually held me accountable to the high standard that would help me grow.

Even when others in our building questioned why I was in certain roles or leading certain endeavors, she remained unwavering. She understood the power of connecting people with opportunities in ways that grew both who I was as a leader, as well as our school as a result. It was the double win.

Your team is full of tremendous people, loaded with potential. That was a confident sentence, wasn't it? Oftentimes, it is a matter of what we look for. You will find what you look for in people. So, look for the good.

On our teams, we have the privilege to build capacity in every person and grow them towards their potential. Certainly, there is a varying degree of effectiveness, because people need to "want" to grow in order to grow. That's a given. But,

> You will find what you look for in people. So, look for the good.

how are we communicating as leaders that we *believe* in each person we serve and are *committed* to growing who they are and their impact on our teams? Do your people feel this from you?

The Multiplication Factor

When it comes to leadership, one of our greatest accomplishments is the result of growing other leaders. Even further, when the leaders we grow then, in turn, develop more leaders. This is where exponential growth happens. And this occurs just as much by the culture you create as it is the strategy you execute and the example you set.

There is no doubt that as high performing leaders, we often have to fight the urge of, "It is just easier for me to do it." Or "If they do it, I will just have to do it over again anyways to my standard." This can be a slippery slope. Because guess what? It probably *is* easier for you to do it. For a while. Until you are burned out, overwhelmed, overstretched, and bitter. Until you truly realize that your ideas may not always be the *best* idea.

When we do this, we close ourselves off from doing the really meaningful work of developing our people, and we limit the multiplication factor. And as leaders, this is what we are commissioned to do. For example, next time something presents itself, rather than focusing on "*How* to?" begin to reframe your thinking and instead ask, "*Who* to?"

A Story from Todd

When I became principal of an elementary campus in Texas, I immediately felt like everything was on me. In most of my experiences observing various leaders, that's what happened. The person at the top carried all the weight and did most of the work. After serving as classroom teacher, I was also carrying a mindset of, "If you want it done right, do it yourself".

Boy was I wrong. My first two years as the campus principal, I led every interview for new potential team additions. I asked the questions, made the decision on hiring or moving on, all of it. As I began to come into my own leadership style and deepen my understanding of the value of those around me and growing them, I realized the amount of untapped brilliance I was missing.

So I began to have conversations with people on my team about considering serving on an interview committee. One where I would be present, but only to listen. One where they would ask the questions. They would provide feedback. They would be part of the decision regarding whom to hire. Immediately I engaged in numerous conversations with several people I wanted on the interview committee. Each conversation ended with that person being floored that they were even considered. It was my opportunity to let them know just how much I valued them, how much they brought to the table, and how their values aligned with the type of people we wanted to add to the team.

You know what happened? The people we began to hire were even more vetted and stronger than those I had ever selected on my own. The perspectives and brilliance of those on the interview committee blew me away with how much better things were when I empowered others to work alongside me instead of just taking it all on myself.

When authentic leaders communicate trust and confidence to those they lead, it limits anxiety and serves as a catapult for their growth. Have you ever had someone say, "Go ahead. I believe in you. Don't worry, I have your back"? There are few things more confidence-boosting than hearing that from your leader.

How Do You View the People You Lead?

How do you feel about the people you lead? Do you love and truly care about them? Or do you simply view them as part of the process by which your school, business, or organization operates? Your first impression might be, "Of course I love and care about them." However, do *they* experience this from you? The reality is, people can tell if you like them or not. They can tell how you feel. They know if you are just tolerating them. They know when something feels forced. We have all been there. We have had a leader who we know wasn't fond of us. They never told us that, of course, but we knew. It was obvious to us.

On the flip side, people can also tell when you are open-hearted towards them. When you pursue relational transparency and are authentic. When they experience this, it lowers anxiety, and creates more trust. It communicates, "I care about you so much, that even at your worst, I will move towards you. Because that's my choice." It helps them feel comfortable taking risks. It allows them the freedom to be themselves. *That* is powerful leadership.

> **Insight from a fellow leader:** *"Relational transparency is the key to building trust with each interaction. As you share information and collaborate with your team, every person participating in the process becomes confident in sharing ideas, emotions, and thoughts. Without transparency as a leader, you create insecurity, anxiety, and distrust."*
> –Joshua Stamper, Training and Development Specialist, *Teach Better*

The Uncomfortable is Worth It

As a leader, you understand the high value of relationships and culture. However, there are inevitably times when situations happen that either need to be addressed or people get hurt. It is in these times that you live and lead from your value system and vulnerability for the sake of your team. It is in these times you truly understand the value in a sincere apology. Because when something has value to you, you will contend for it. Even the uncomfortable is worth it.

A Story from Tyler

A few years ago, I had to make an unpopular decision that affected a number of people. As a result, one of our employees did not like the decision that I made, and I could tell. Do you know how some people can hide their feelings, and others aren't as successful? This person fit into the latter category. I could feel the disconnection creeping in, and I knew that it would have just been easier for me to justify my decision and point the finger at the illegitimate reason this person was upset. It would have been easy for me to broker the disconnection and allow the two of us to simply remain at arm's length from each other.

However, at that moment I had a choice. We continually discuss as a team our core values of working together as a team, seeing the best in each other, and having each other's backs. It was my responsibility as a leader to take ownership of our relationship. So, I simply refused to let it get awkward. I walked down to their room the next day and asked if we could chat. They said, "Sure."

I proceeded to say, "I know you don't love the decision I made, but do you know what I do love? This. Our relationship that we have spent years building. This situation will pass, but I want our relationship to last for a long time."

I smiled and made my way back down to my office. Two days later, there was a note in my mailbox. It said, "Tyler, thank you for stopping by. I really appreciate you and I am thankful for you."

Authentic leaders always move towards. They always protect. They always build. They lead from *who they are*, not the circumstances they are in.

Water the Ground You are Planted In

Think about your role as a leader. What is in your hands right now? Who have you been entrusted to lead and grow? Leadership expert John Maxwell said, "What we appreciate appreciates, and what we depreciate depreciates" (Maxwell, 2022).

Think of it like this: Picture a "fixer-upper" house on a block of houses. If you are willing to see what could be, and put in the time, effort, and care to bring it to fruition, what happens to the value of that home? It appreciates. Similarly, when we as leaders are willing to see the potential inside of others, and are willing to spend the time, speak truth, and provide healthy opportunities for their growth, they "appreciate" towards their potential. It is a beautiful thing. Just like the saying goes, "The grass is greener where you water it."

Let's take it a step further. When you take that "fixer-upper" house and increase its appraised value from $200,000 to $320,000, what does it do to the rest of the home values in that neighborhood? It increases *their* values as well! Imagine what intentionally investing in the people you serve to a greater

> Reflect: Who do you need to invest into in a different way? What will that look like?
> _____

capacity will do for your team, your department, or your organization? It's about seeing the best in those we lead, so that we can lead them to be their best.

Relational Equity

As Jimmy Casas emphasizes in his book, "Culturize" (Casas, 2017), we as leaders need to invest in the "Three Rs" on a daily basis: relationships, relationships, relationships. Your relationships are like your GPS for those you lead. Staying connected not only strengthens trust and helps unite your common vision, but also provides you with information to best serve them and their strengths on your team. Below are some ways to build relational equity with those you lead:

1. **Be Present** - Simply put, this means to *be engaged*. Wherever you are, be all there. Keep your cell phone away during meetings, don't check your email while someone is in your office. Make eye contact, smile, and be genuinely thankful to be in that moment with them, even if your world is pulling on you from other directions. They know you are busy, so doing this communicates, "You are important to me."

2. **Be Interested** - Be sincerely interested in the things that interest them. Lean in and actively listen. Ask good questions. You don't need to carpool to an antique show with someone just because they brought it up in a conversation, but they should at least know that if it is important to them, it is interesting and important to you. Just as importantly, remember the personal stories they share so you can follow up and ask questions later to let them know what they shared was important to you.

3. **Be Consistent** - As an authentic leader, it is so important that our actions align with our words. Being consistent looks like following

up when you say you will, apologizing when you need to (and you most certainly will), and staying true to your value system. People should never have to question which "you" they are going to get. Even in challenging situations, they should be able to know how you would respond, even without you there, because they are so intimately aware of your values that you lead by and your organization's values that you are committed to.

4. **Be Powerful** - This means that you are responsible for managing your relationships and the pull on your mental bandwidth. You can only give so much of yourself as a leader, and so if you are feeling drained, utilize self-awareness and take a step away to recharge. That is completely OK. Ten minutes with the door closed in your office can do wonders. You want to bring the best of yourself to those you lead, not a sharp, edgy version. You don't ever want a simple question from one of your colleagues to be the "straw that broke the camel's back," because that could result in hurt relationships, when in actuality the responsibility was on you to manage yourself and your emotions more effectively.

The Power of Empowerment

This is one of the most incredible yet misunderstood words in leadership. As author and leader Craig Groeschel states, "Empowerment is not simply delegating tasks. Empowerment is the delegation of authority." He goes on to say, "The strength of your team is not a reflection of what you control. It is the reflection of who you empower" (Groeschel, 2018).

As authentic leaders, the values, transparency, positive psychological capital (hope, optimism, resilience, self-efficacy), and trust that we foster can all be developed in the people we lead. Much of the first part of this book truly spoke to our own personal development and the resulting byproduct of developing this in our people, based on who we are. However, when it comes to empowerment, this takes the work to roll up our sleeves and truly grow and develop people into who they have potential to become.

The word "empower" actually means to give someone authority, to equip, to qualify, and to give someone the means to achieve something. Those are some powerful definitions! Is there anyone on your team that you have "disqualified" over the years? If so, use this as an encouragement to begin viewing your people based on how you are going to equip them to impact your organization and your vision.

This chapter was written intentionally, because if we don't truly love the people we lead and invest in them relationally, it is going to be hard to trust them with something that is important and valuable to you. Furthermore, if you say, "Well, they need to prove themselves," but view them through their shortcomings rather than their potential, they never will. Again, this isn't always easy, but the work is always worth it.

> **Insight from a leader:** *"For me it's all about relationships! Those around you will not bring out their best or see their potential unless they feel valued, support and trust you. Building relationships that allow this takes intentionally and have to be genuine. Once relationships are built, you continue to foster and value them, then you are intentional about seeing the strengths in those around you. So many do not see their own strengths and potential. As leaders, it is a must to be intentional and vocal to those around us. Tell them how great they are, emphasize their strengths and value the assets they bring to your organization."*
> –Ross Braun, Principal

80/20 Rule of Empowerment

There is an 80/20 rule for just about anything. Finances, business, priorities, etc. However, for the purposes of this book, the 80/20 rule refers to empowerment. As leaders, we need to begin empowering and equipping more of our people, delegate more decision making, and allow for individual autonomy.

The 80/20 rule is this: If there is someone on your team who can accomplish something 80% as effectively as you can, *and* they are teachable, let them run with it by saying to them, "I love it. Run with it. Here's what I want you to do: go find two other people that you feel are teachable and would add value to this and bring them alongside you."

Now, you have three people empowered on your team and growing in their capacity to impact your organization. Plus, the first person is leading two other people. Be sure to offer support, show interest and excitement, and communicate confidence along the way. Don't just disappear. This is empowerment at its finest.

The Language of Empowerment

There are many phrases that foster trust and confidence when it comes to empowering others. A few powerful ones are, "I trust you," "You decide on this one," and "What do you think?" It reframes the conversation from looking at you as the leader for the answer, to communicating that you believe in what is inside them to solve it.

A Story from Tyler

"What do you think?"

I remember the first time I asked this to one of my new employees, in response to a question she asked me about a scenario she encountered. She stared back at me for a second. And then she repeated her question. I simply smiled, and asked her again, "What do YOU think we should do?"

She slowly cracked a smile. She then shared her idea—well thought out, clearly articulated, and passionate. So, we *went* with it.

To this day, I don't remember the question she asked me, but I do remember the way she stood a little taller in my office doorway as she passionately detailed her idea that she was about to go hit a home run with.

Her idea, not mine (which was better than mine, anyways).

"What do you think?" Four simple words. Four words that communicate: Trust, belief, confidence, and commitment. When we BELIEVE in people, we bring out the BEST in people.

Re-Writing the Leadership Script

In the opening pages of this book, we revealed that less than 50% of people actually trusted their leaders to do the right thing. As a leader, this hurts to read. Although each of us falls short of our own standards of excellence occasionally and are far from perfect, we have the opportunity to change the narrative of leadership. Not by increasing our productivity or maximizing the effectiveness of programmatic initiatives, but in the way we *love and care about people*. In the way we see the good that is inside them and encourage them to move from their comfort zone to their growth zone. And in the way we live and lead from our deeply held core values and authentic selves. This is possible. And it is our hope that you are catching more and more of a glimpse of the authentic leader you were created to be.

NEXT STEPS:

1. Which of the four ideas of building relational equity most resonated with you, and why? Which one did you identify as an area of growth? Who will hold you accountable for that growth?

2. When was the last time you felt empowered by someone who is a leader in your life? What did they do exactly to make you feel that way? Write down your experience and reflect on the words you put on paper (or typed).

CHAPTER 8

~

Life by Design

As a high-performing leader, there are endless demands for your time, your focus, and your energy. So, how do you gain clarity on what healthy balance looks and feels like in your life? More importantly, how do you implement a strategy that *schedules your priorities* so that you can *show up* with excellence in every area of your life?

It doesn't happen by accident, and it isn't a one-time choice. Living powerfully and intentionally is about refocusing your mind daily, committing to who and what matters most to you, and bringing your best self into every aspect of your life.

We have spent years researching and interviewing leaders who long to live authentically and stay true to the life they desire. The reality is, many of these leaders are overwhelmed by their responsibilities and feel like they have little left to give to their most important relationships and priorities. They feel weighed down by the demands on their time and they feel guilty that they aren't showing up for those who matter most and that all they have to give to them are the leftovers.

Can you think of an area in your life that you aren't showing up as your best self? Are you disconnected from the relationships in your life? Do you wrestle with feelings of guilt and regret when you lay your head on your pillow at night? If so, you *don't have to live that way!* You do not have to choose your career OR your friends and family. You can lead with excellence and pursue your passions, while also living and loving fully in your family and personal life. No matter your situation or circumstance, you can create the life you desire. It's within your reach.

> **Insight from a fellow leader:** *"Working to be an authentic leader is a daily exercise. I practice the miracle morning daily routine to prepare myself to serve others. By reflecting and going over my goals in the morning, I love how I can show up as a better person for those I do life with."*
> –Lynmara Colon, Director

Bringing Alignment

As a leader, there is no denying that the pull on your life never stops. The to-do list truly does never end. From emails to deadlines, your responsibilities oftentimes are not compartmentalized during your daily work hours. However, if you are not intentional in defining your priorities (non-negotiables) and fail to create a plan for how they will show up in your life, your moments will instead be filled with something else that takes its place, leaving you feeling the guilt, disconnection, and overwhelm of not living the life you want.

No matter your leadership role, season of life, or situation, it is vital to build your life in a way that fosters personal growth, cultivates your most important relationships, and stewards your career and professional responsibilities. You do not have to choose work or home. But, to *win* both, you need strategy, alignment, and intentionality. When these are out of alignment, you get burned out, lose your vision, and sacrifice important relationships. How many times have you felt that pit in your stomach because you knew you weren't present or fully engaged in your life, all for something that, in comparison, paled in importance?

Or maybe you have missed moments that you know you can never have back, and vow that you will make a change, yet the demands and responsibilities just keep coming.

A Story from Todd

I'll never forget the moment that my wife looked at me and said, "Something has to give. It's obvious how unhappy you are and I'm worried."

I had convinced myself that no one could see the depths at which I was feeling burnt out and broken. But of course, my spouse knew all along. This was a point in my career when the workload became unbearable, the expectations impossible, my supervisors did nothing but demean, and I felt worthless and like a failure. I wasn't defining my non-negotiables. I wasn't setting boundaries. I lost my vision, my hope, my compass. I allowed the expectations and endless lists to overrun my life and did nothing to take care of myself.

It was in that simple moment of my wife telling me that something had to give that I was finally smacked across the face with the reality of where I had allowed myself to end up. That was the conversation that allowed me to recalibrate and make some decisions that were hard, but better, for my own health and for the health of my family. And looking back now, I couldn't be happier with those decisions. I'm sure my wife would also tell you that she knew what she was talking about the whole time, too. Thank God she spoke into me and that I listened.

If things feel out of alignment for you, now is your time, and today is your day, to create and establish your life around that which is most important to you. So, be filled with hope today. The very fact that you are reading this is a testament to your courage and commitment to live well, love well, and lead your life well.

> **Insight from a fellow leader:** *"Leaders have a lot on their plate and taking care of themselves is an important part of what keeps us up and running. Some ways I keep myself organized and energized are weightlifting 4-6 times per week after work as well as meal prepping for the week on Sunday nights to always have a healthy meal to fuel my body during the day. I have also put my mental health first by talking to my doctor about my anxiety and receiving medication that has empowered me to take control of anxiety attacks when they arise. Additionally, I have a partner, family, and friends that have been my rocks throughout my professional careers to support me through the hard days and celebrate with me on the good days. By taking care of my body, mind, and surrounding myself with a strong support system, I've been able to foster healthy systems of support to keep myself from burning out."*
> –Shane Saeed, Instructional Coach

The Value and Necessity of Boundaries

The world around us consists of numerous boundaries. We see it everywhere–fences, signs, walls–and those boundaries are used to clarify ownership and responsibility. Furthermore, just as our physical world consists of boundaries, our *lives* do as well. These boundaries serve the important purpose of not only keeping the good *in*, but the unhealthy *out*.

Think of your life as a property, which subsequently has property lines. Your property lines allow you to know where you are responsible, and, in turn, where you are in charge of protecting what matters most to you in your life. This can be tremendously difficult in leadership, as we often take on the false responsibility of feeling like we need to be all things to all people. Not only is this unrealistic, but it is unsustainable, and usually results in compromising our focus on what is truly important.

As leaders, we frequently overextend ourselves due to a *lack* of boundaries, which is generally a result of not clearly defining our "yes" and our "no." We fear that we will let others down, diminish our reputation, or even believe the lie that we must model "overwork" to prove our worth or credibility. Unfortunately, this is not the message of authenticity, but rather of fear or insecurity. Therefore, the byproduct of this can result in guilt, stress, and regret. However, remember–you are not created to be all things to all people!

In Havilah Cunnington's book, *I Do Boundaries* (2020), she talks about picturing your life like a yard. Then, ask yourself, are there any holes in your fence or shrubs in your yard that don't belong? In other words, are there areas where you have compromised your boundaries due to not clearly communicating your "yes" or "no", or are there commitments and/or relationships that have crept into your life that you know aren't healthy but which you have settled and compromised?

Moving forward, use this analogy to make powerful, intentional choices to protect the important things and prioritize your commitments. Most of all, imagine being able to communicate your priorities, live them out, and stop feeling bad about that. Boundaries are not only healthy, but essential in building authenticity as a leader.

The Priority Pyramid

The graphic below outlines the five components of creating and sustaining a purposeful life by design. Each component of the priority pyramid reflects a different aspect of your life, all of which deserves a proportionate amount of your time. However, the emphasis is on the word *proportionate*.

There is no doubt that your career and leadership responsibilities encompass more raw time in your week than anything else. But, your life is not solely measured in minutes. It is measured in value. In being present. In being engaged and committed in those moments that you DO spend *leading yourself, living your purpose, loving your people, and leading your team.* This is a life by design—and this is the life you are capable of living.

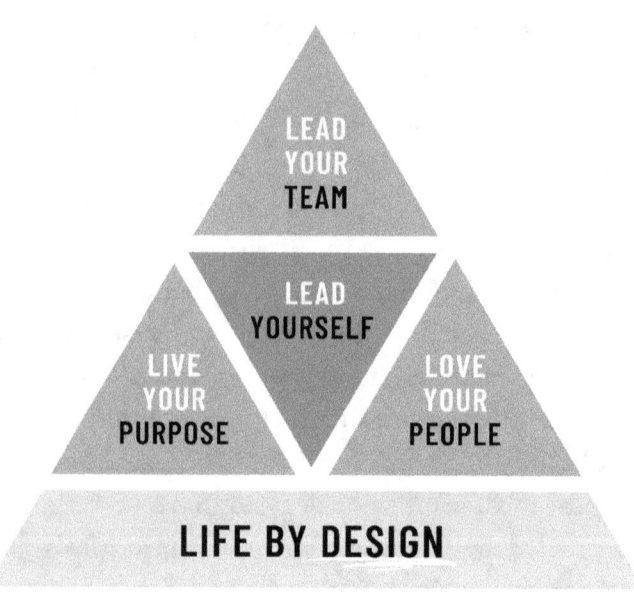

In each subsequent section of this chapter, you will find examples of what each component may encompass. These are examples, but they are meant to help you reflect on how you desire for them to look and how you plan to show up in each area of your life. Maybe you have a specific example in mind, or perhaps you are looking at the "big picture" at the moment. That's fine for the time being, but the goal is to be targeted, specific, and intentional with how and in what ways you commit to engaging each component of the pyramid on a daily basis.

TIP: If you don't know where to start, close your eyes, take a breath, and feel where the greatest pull is inside you. Where do you feel guilt or urgency—those areas in which you haven't shown up but deserve the best version of yourself? Where do you wish you felt more peace? Here is your starting point.

This will all make sense as you work your way through the components, but it is important that you are honest with yourself so that you can reestablish your vision for your life, reclaim your priorities, and be more effective in those areas of need.

In working through this chapter, you will find clarity about *what* aspects of your life need refining, *how* you are going to show up in those areas, and *when* it will show up in your schedule. You will be incorporating different components of authenticity discussed earlier in this book and applying it to your life in practical ways. As a byproduct, you will strengthen your relationships, find your peace, and live with purpose.

1. LEAD YOURSELF

As you can see on the priority pyramid, Leading Yourself is centrally located and is the cornerstone of the pyramid. Regardless of your leadership capacity, your relationships, or even your aspirations, you must lead yourself well *first*, in order to bring your *best* self into every other area of your life. At its core, *leading* yourself well is *caring* for yourself well with honesty, authenticity, and self-discipline. Not from just a physical standpoint, but also mentally, emotionally, and spiritually.

Are you led by your thoughts, feelings, and emotions? Do you find that a stressful conversation or bad news throws the remainder of your day and evening into an internal tailspin? Or are you intentional to renew your mind each day and build routines into your life that foster positive, powerful thinking and perspective?

Building this could look like taking time to journal each morning to process through your internal dialogue as mentioned earlier in the book, or spending five minutes in a gratitude journal each day to cultivate thankfulness. This could also look like spending time in prayer and/or meditation each day to reset your focus and heart. The act of just finding time to sit in silence grows hope, purpose, and peace inside of you.

Additionally, an often-avoided practice of high-performing leaders is living in relational transparency. However, when you invite others into your life as a support system, they may have insight into your "blind spots" that can, in fact, be holding you back from living freely and fully. Who in your life can you trust to have those real and honest conversations with you?

Another important component of leading yourself well is developing and fostering a strong level of self-awareness. Think of yourself as a car as discussed in Chapter 3, and your dashboard as your indicators of your health. Fostering self-awareness helps you stay aware of any lights flashing on your dashboard. If you find yourself struggling in an area, perhaps it is an indication of that area needing some attention.

Too often, leaders ignore their dashboard and push themselves to the limit. When you run out of fuel, overheat your engine—or worse—no one wins. Especially not those closest and most important to you. And, unlike a car, you can't be replaced. Authentic leaders prioritize self-awareness so they can live and give as the healthiest version of themselves.

So, what does leading yourself well look like in your life from a practical standpoint? What are specific things that you will do to ensure that you are growing, having the hard conversations with yourself, and leading yourself with care and excellence? Fill out the section below with real commitments and actionable items (e.g., Wake up at 5:00 a.m. daily to journal and pray, etc.). When we put things into writing we're much more likely to follow through:

Your Priority (What)	Your Action (How)	Your Schedule (When)
Example: Rest	*In Bed by 10:30 PM*	*Sunday - Thursday*

2. LIVE YOUR PURPOSE

It is no secret that pursuing your purpose, or your *"why"*, is essential to living a life of quality and meaning. However, identifying your "why" is one thing; keeping your purpose and vision alive inside of you on a daily basis is another. Both of us have spent years of our lives battling the internal dialogue that "purpose = achievement." When we accomplished or achieved something, we had value and it affirmed who we were. Unfortunately, this created unrest and undue pressure on ourselves, leaving us feeling unfulfilled, unsatisfied, and lacking peace.

Truth is that high-performing leaders oftentimes exhibit many great characteristics of pursuing their purpose. They are driven, motivated, and disciplined. They often feel the need to be pursuing a goal. They live from a mindset of, "If you aren't growing, you're dying." While this can be an admirable quality, when not managed well, it can lead to anxiety, fear, and unrest.

In the journey shared above, we finally discovered that it wasn't achievement that we were really desiring–it was *progress and meaning*. This can be a fine art of balance for leaders, who are results-oriented by nature. This is why many leaders struggle with connection at home or in their personal relationships. Cultivating those relationships, doing the work behind the scenes, and showing up even when it's hard can lack the feeling of immediate "reward" or "accomplishment" for leaders. Because of this, it is vital to keep your purpose alive inside you every day. Ask yourself these questions:

What brings me true joy in life?
What do I truly long for?
I feel fulfilled when….

Chances are, it isn't meeting your deadlines or answering emails in a timely fashion. Most likely, it comes back to those true priorities in your life. The WHO and WHAT that matters most.

As you pursue living your purpose, building in time for self-reflection and self-discovery is key. Taking time to search inward, asking yourself questions, identifying limiting beliefs, and replacing them with empowering beliefs will help you live in the driver seat of your life, not simply being controlled by your emotions, guilt, or negative inner dialogue.

Another component of living your purpose is to *focus on what you have*. What blessings in your life are right in front of you? What have you been given in life that you have the privilege to steward well? What relationships or opportunities are in your hands that will allow you to be your best self? Living with an abundance mindset of gratitude, perspective, and meaning will help you unwrap clarity, joy, and peace in your life. It will make living your purpose an *exciting journey*, rather than a stressful goal.

Finally, growing in self-awareness and discovering your true needs is an important aspect of living your purpose. Lack of awareness of your own needs can leave you feeling a false sense of purpose, or even one based on others' expectations of you. Learning about yourself helps you identify what motivates you, gives you a sense of purpose, and fulfills your innermost needs. Ever heard of the Enneagram? This might be a great place to start. The Enneagram is a personality indicator tool that can help identify how you view and interpret the world in one of nine ways. It's an incredibly helpful resource for understanding yourself and what drives you.

So, what does living your purpose look like in your life from a practical standpoint? What are specific things that you will do to ensure that you are staying true to who you are, pursuing fulfillment, and finding peace in your progress? Fill out the section below with real commitments and actionable items (e.g., daily focusing on progress rather than achievement, starting a gratitude journal to foster thankfulness and peace, growing in self-awareness through resources like the Enneagram.)

Your Priority (What)	Your Action (How)	Your Schedule (When)
Example: Cultivating Thankfulness	*Gratitude Journal*	*Daily with my morning coffee*

3. LOVE YOUR PEOPLE

Mother Teresa once said, *"If you want to change the world, go home and love your family."* Truer words have never been spoken. Before you continue skimming down through this section, stop and reflect on that statement for a moment. Your greatest leadership is actually inside the front doors of your home. The legacy that you will leave—the greatest fulfillment you will find and the most impact that you can have—is in loving your people well.

What relationships in your life mean the most to you? Perhaps it's your husband or wife; maybe it's your children or grandchildren; maybe it's a parent, or other close relationships.

> Your greatest leadership is actually inside the front doors of your home.

Whoever it is, they deserve your best. They are the ones for you to *show up for* each and every day.

If you take away anything from this chapter, hear this: too many leaders get to the end of their life and regret not spending more time with those who matter most. Too many leaders look back and wish they had been more present, more engaged, and more giving of their time to the people in their life that were the most valuable. We have spoken to countless leaders who have openly admitted to sacrificing their families for the sake of their leadership roles and responsibilities. They felt weighed down and stuck, and their relationships paid the price for it. Years later, they still live with the guilt of not being present in the most important moments—which oftentimes can be the littlest, simplest ones.

In the age of email accessibility on your phone, it is easy (and sometimes expected) to never fully unplug. However, this is a thief of your time, your attention, and your engagement with your most valuable people.

Healthy boundaries protect your time and empower you to be present when it matters. Maybe it's putting your phone up on the fridge when you get home for a couple of hours. Maybe when you are out to dinner, you keep it in your pocket, rather than on the table with you. Whatever it is, it is important that you model this for your families, children, relationships, etc. who are most important in your life, because oftentimes it's not what you say that speaks volumes, but what they see you doing.

Mother Teresa lived in a simpler time, but the premise of her words still rings true. This is why clear priorities help guide you. Create a plan for how you will be present and engaged when you walk in your doors at night, or when you are with those who matter most. The bottom line is, every person desires to show up and love their people well. And most people battle with guilt for not doing it as well as they would like. It's time to change the narrative. Re-establish how you will be engaged and present in your relationships. Today is the day to love your people, lead your family, and create the peace, joy, and fulfillment of living connected with those who are closest to you.

So, what does this area look like in your life from a practical standpoint? Fill out the section below with real commitments and actionable items. (e.g., "unplugging" when you get home, eating dinner together as a family, weekly date nights, calling parents once a week, etc.)

Your Priority (What)	Your Action (How)	Your Schedule (When)
Example: Prioritizing my wife	*Date Nights*	*Every other Friday*

4. LEAD YOUR TEAM

As a leader, you have most likely gotten to where you are today because of hard work, sacrifice, and utilizing your gifts and abilities to add value to those around you. You have dedicated yourself to refining your skills, growing your influence, and taking the road less traveled that many people aren't willing to navigate. This is because you know there is potential and greatness inside you, and you are driven to ensure that you leave your mark on the world in a meaningful way.

As amazing (and fulfilling) as this is, many times it comes with subtle compromises. Your leadership responsibilities require much from you, often in the form of long hours, open access to your calendar and schedule, others expecting you to answer when they call/text/email, and emotional and mental demands for your "A-Game" at all times.

You undoubtedly want to lead others with excellence each day. But, without leading yourself well, leaders can quickly slide into emotional scarcity, which leads to burnout, stress, and being completely overwhelmed. We have worked with many leaders who lacked healthy boundaries, sacrificed self-care, and ultimately drove themselves into survival mode—both in their personal lives and in their leadership (including us at times).

In order to lead a healthy life, you must live healthy habits. You've most likely heard the saying, "You can't pour from an empty cup." This can be applied to every area of your life, but in regard to your leadership, it is your responsibility to not only stay mentally, physically, and emotionally nourished and balanced, but to also model this for those you lead. In fact, one of the greatest gifts you can give people you lead is to model what a healthy life and healthy boundaries actually look like. When they see their leader stressed out, responding to emails all hours of the night, burning the candle at both ends, and living in scarcity, it sends a negative message to the team and actually creates an unspoken expectation for others to do the same. The goal of an authentic leader is to not only live and lead healthily, but to also develop this culture in their business or organization.

So, what does managing this priority of *leading your team* look like? How does establishing healthy work/career boundaries actually play out in your life? Maybe it is committing to not checking your email after a certain time. For example, there is nothing worse than reading a negative or heavy email at 9:00 p.m., only to throw the rest of your night off, steal your peace, and consume you for the remainder of the evening. This can rob you of being "present" in the evening and *loving your people* well.

Additionally, when you don't respond to emails at all hours of the night, it sends the message that you are not available and accessible 24/7. If you absolutely need to respond to an email for your own peace of mind, perhaps set the "send" time to 6:00 a.m. the next morning. Another example of managing yourself in this area is to bring closure at the end of your workday and create a to-do list for the following day so that you can make the mental transition from work to home. If you leave work with too many "open boxes" in your mind with no plan to address them, they will ping around in your mind until you do.

This doesn't deny the work that needs to be done, but it gives you a plan and permission to be present for those who matter most when you leave the office. Remember, if you pass away today, your job will be posted tomorrow. But, there is only one you for your family and those most important to you.

So, what do these areas look like in your life from a practical standpoint? Fill out the tier below with real commitments and actionable items. (e.g., not checking emails after 9:00 p.m. etc.)

Your Priority (What)	Your Action (How)	Your Schedule (When)
Example: Helping myself leave work at work	Daily "end of day" to-do list for the next day	Before I leave work each day

5. LIFE BY DESIGN

You've established your priorities. You've had honest conversations with yourself. You know the internal work that needs done. And, you are ready to say goodbye to the guilt, pressure, and overwhelm that tries to convince you that you are not good enough, stuck, and have no way out. So, now is the time to put it all together—now you create your *Life by Design.*

Living a life by design isn't rocket science. It isn't a concept that is earth-shattering. But if it was easy, everyone would do it. Living a life by design is about being intentional to make sure that your priorities SHOW UP in your life when you want them to, and that you protect those things above all else. The surface level work has been done—you have established *what* you need to do. You know ways that you need to take care of yourself and *lead yourself* well. You know the areas that you need to get back on track with, in terms of *living your purpose*. You are excited to *love your people* the way they deserve—with you being present and engaged in their lives. And you know the tweaks you need to make in the way you *lead your team*.

Now is the time to establish *when* and *how* you will do these things. This is the foundation of the pyramid. Without this, your great ideas or noble aspirations will never happen in your life, which will ultimately lead to greater guilt and anxiety. Creating systems, schedules, and routines in your life will lead you to the freedom you desire, so that you can feel in control of your life, stop existing, *and* really start living.

You are successful as a leader because you have an operational strategy that you implement with precision. You plan, execute, refine, and repeat in order to move forward the vision for your business and organization. Now, let's do this with your life.

As you wrap up this chapter, don't let the opportunity pass you by to build the priorities into your life that you have identified and defined above for each of the four main components of the pyramid. Go back and write them down elsewhere, where they can serve as a visual reminder. Perhaps even take some time to further expand on each of the areas. Identify *what* your priority is that you commit to protecting, how you plan on it showing up in your life, and *when* it will be found on your calendar. Be targeted, specific, and actionable. Nothing vague and nothing abstract. Be intentional.

Your Plan into Reality

Putting your plan on paper brings substance and reality to your goals. Doing this provides you with the tools necessary to carve out your priorities with intention and shape your daily commitments. From there, populate your calendar so that you can *schedule your priorities* in your life, rather than *prioritizing your schedule*.

Remember, living from your priorities does not just happen—it requires daily intention and action. Stay true to the course you are charting and celebrate your wins, both big and small. Build momentum in your life, and feel the abundance and prosperity that you are meant to live in. You deserve to live as your best self, and those around you deserve the best you as well. This is your most important leadership commitment.

NEXT STEPS:

1. When reflecting on the four main components of the pyramid, which do you most identify as a strength of yours? What evidence in your life makes you feel that it is a strength?

2. When it comes to a piece of the pyramid you want to grow in, which one do you gravitate towards? Why do you feel that is an area of growth for you? What steps will you take to develop in this area?

CHAPTER 9

Ground Zero–Your Most Important Leadership

If you want to change the world, go home and love your family.
-Mother Teresa

These words are most certainly worth repeating. In fact, this topic is so important to us that we wanted to dedicate a specific chapter to it. Your family is your most important leadership. End of story. There will never be a better investment, nor will there ever be a more important meeting than the time that you spend inside the front doors of your home. However, as you are building authenticity in your life, it is vital to remember that it is not simply the minutes of your time that matter, it is how you show up that matters.

A Story from Tyler

I will never forget the night. My wife and I were both feeling disconnected, and it was evident. I was building a case in my mind as to why things were the way they were, and it clearly wasn't on

---

my end of things (boy was I wrong). In my mind, I had clearly mapped out all of the precipitating events that led to our tension, and as I was ready to unpack it all, Stacey spoke up from across the room.

She looked up at me and said, "At work you are this great leader. I hear people all the time say how patient and kind you are. How you work through conflict and connect with people. How you show empathy and compassion. Yet, I don't see that Tyler here. Why do they get that Tyler, and we don't at home?"

Her words went through me like a cannonball. She was right. I was giving the best of myself at work, and when I came home I took my foot off of the gas pedal. I lacked the patience or empathy that my wife and kids deserved, and oftentimes brought a tired and stressed version of myself home. I was giving them what was *left* of me.

As painful as it was to hear, this was the feedback I needed. My family deserved the *best* of me. There is one husband for my wife and one dad for my kids. I scrolled through examples in my mind and put myself in my baby girl's shoes as she looked for her daddy's smile and attention. I put myself in my boys' shoes as they eagerly awaited to play soccer in the backyard with Dad. I put myself in my wife's shoes as she simply needed some support with the kids and a loving, patient rock to lean on and partner with.

There needed to be a recalibration. Are things perfect every day? No - because life with 4 kids under the age of 11 rarely are. But it is through these lenses that I have committed my life to live and love my family first and foremost.

An Integrated LIfe

If this story resonates with you at all, it is most likely because of the battle to live a truly integrated life. This means being the same person, no matter where you are. It is easy to lead at work with a sense of urgency, because who you are and what you do are on display on a daily basis and the stakes are high. However, inside your home, the stakes are even higher. Because who you are and what you do imprints on the hearts and lives of those closest to you. This is your legacy, and this is what builds identity and security in your children, and support and connection with your spouse.

To lead an integrated life looks like bringing together all the major elements of your professional and personal life–your authentic self–so that you can be the same person everywhere all the time. This is about as clear a definition of authentic as you can get. That is the YOU that people close to you need.

However, as Bill George defines in "Discover Your True North," *integration* is not the same as work/life *balance (George, 2015, p. 159)*. While balance implies keeping things in equilibrium or compartmentalized, integrating your life prioritizes what is most important to you, and helps ensure that you are embedding the same values, goals, and character in *all* aspects of your life.

> **Insight from a fellow leader:** *"My best should be for my wife and kids. But there are times when they get my worst—which is at the end of the day when I am tired, stressed, etc. from the pressures of a long day at work. So, I try to intentionally plan for more extended breaks from work (vacation, etc.) when I have more dedicated time just for family. Additionally, over the years, I was very intentional about including my family in my work (especially when my children were younger). They regularly traveled with me to games, were ball persons for our home games, and "hung out" when I was running practices.*

We also regularly had our players in our home, so my family became part of my work as I invested in my team."
–Matthew Webb, Director of Athletics at Houghton University

The Trap

The reality is, more well-intentioned leaders fall victim to the trap of not prioritizing their time and giving their best to what matters most than we want to admit. We've all seen it—the cliche movie where the Fortune 500 parent is too busy to play catch with their son because they're too busy on work calls, or isn't able to leave the office on time to catch their daughter's school recital. However, this storyline plays out in subtle ways far too often in our homes and lives, resulting in the sting of laying our heads on our pillows at night, knowing we weren't fully present.

If you are reading this book, you are most likely serving in some sort of leadership capacity. As a result, there are responsibilities of your role that inevitably wage war on your time outside of office hours. In our world that is more connected than ever before, the expectation of engagement and connectedness to work during your evenings and weekends has followed the same trajectory line. However, today is a reminder that your identity is not in what you do for your job. Your identity is in who you are—a father, a mother, a spouse, a grandparent, a sibling, a son, a daughter, a friend, etc. There is only one of you—and *your world* is counting on you.

Let's take a common business term, ROI, or "Return on Investment" and apply it to your life. Think about those big "buckets" in your life—your professional life, your friendships, your personal life, and your family. Where is the greatest value and return on your investment? It is unequivocally your family that is most important. And as a result, we must daily assess if we are making the right deposits and investments into those relationships that will go far deeper and last longer than the eye can see.

If this applies to you in any way, let today be your reset. Have grace for yourself, forgive yourself, and let this confirmation be your permission to take a look at your life with fresh vision and strategy to create healthy rhythms and commitments that will enable you to give your best to the places that matter most.

> Don't fall into the trap of, "As soon as I _____, then I'll _____." Your family needs you to love and lead them today.
>
> _____

You won't be perfect at this, none of us are. But the important part is making a daily decision to continue working towards your best self.

Lead With Your Life

Country singer Rodney Atkins' song, "Watching You," (Atkins, 2006) depicts so clearly the weight of responsibility that we have to model for our children the values and life we desire for them to live. As the chorus of the song goes:

> He said, "I've been watching you, dad, ain't that cool?
> I'm your buckaroo, I wanna be like you
> And eat all my food, and grow as tall as you are
> We got cowboy boots and camo pants
> Yeah, we're just alike, hey, ain't we dad?
> I wanna do everything you do
> So I've been watching you"

Of course, if you know the song, Randy Atkins begins by having some not-so-positive responses to situations that even include a four-letter word that his son later repeats, because he saw his dad do it. Then later on, after a moment of realization that his life is on display for his family, he bows his head and asks for strength. The song goes on to share that later on that night his son bowed his head to pray before bed. When asked where he learned to pray like that, his son replied, "I've been watching you, Dad."

Will we be perfect? Far from it. But their eyes are watching, and their ears are listening, even when we don't realize it. The subtle non-verbal responses to adversity, the mini teachable moments of integrity that are taught by example, rather than with words, and the precious connections our children make regarding the value of relationships and family will echo in their hearts and minds long after we are gone. This is why our most important leadership starts at home.

Build What Matters, Not What's Easy

The most impactful team you will ever invest in is your family. And unlike your leadership in your career, there is no replacement for your children or other close relationships in your life. You can't delegate that to anyone. That is why we must be committed in every way to investing with our whole hearts in these relationships.

In your professional life, if there is a gap in effectiveness in an area that needs your attention, you will be quick to strategize, plan, and tackle it head on. However, far too many marriages and relationships suffer as a result of not doing the same at home and simply existing from days, to weeks, and even years. Nurturing, growing, and sowing into your family takes intentionality and hard work. Every day. It's not always easy. You'll make quite a few mistakes. And that is why so many people have regrets. Remember, what is easy is rarely what matters, but what takes work is most always worth it.

Humility and Sacrifice

When we lead in a professional setting, it generally consists of others responding to our requests and directives, based on their roles on our teams. However, leading and loving inside our homes looks much different. We all know that kids are messy little people and have their own wills and opinions, many times in opposition to ours as parents. Additionally, building connection and growing your relationship with your partner is one that requires tremendous humility and sacrifice, even if you feel you are right at times.

This is because the goal is connection and growth. Not to be *right*, but to understand one another. And, no one knows us, our tendencies, and our shortcomings better than our loved ones and those closest to you. Talk about vulnerability at an entirely different level. As a result, the greater degree that we posture our heart in humility to grow together, learn each other's needs, and respond accordingly, the further we can move forward together in our collective vision.

Family Values

Just as you have organizational core values and collective beliefs at work, it is even more important to establish these in your home. Who are you as a family? How do you respond to adversity and challenges? When there is disagreement, what action is taken to resolve the situation? What does love and accountability look like, played out in a practical manner? What does generosity and selflessness look like? What is most important to you as a family? How do you talk about these things? How do you exemplify these things?

These are all examples of questions that we can answer for our teams that we lead at work, but ones that often go unestablished in our homes. If you have a spouse and/or children at home, take the time to sit down together and have open conversations with each person's input to establish your core values as a family. Then, write them down and display them for everyone to see. When there is an issue or situation, you now have a collective belief system and culture by which you move forward. *This* is leading inside of your home. *This* is impacting your world in a way that leaves a legacy.

Our Family Values:

Value	Definition
Example: Quality Time	*We eat dinner together as a family and have weekly game / movie nights*
Example: Teamwork	*We pitch in, support one another, and have each other's backs if someone needs help*
Value 1:	Definition:
Value 2:	Definition:
Value 3:	Definition:

Living Your Legacy

Our time on earth is finite and precious. Consequently, so are our most valuable relationships. In life, we have been given a gift and opportunity to invest ourselves into those we love in order to help grow them into their fullest potential and live fruitful lives, marked by their own legacies they will one day leave.

However, as easy as it is to get caught up in our daily routines and rhythms, it is important that we take time to reflect with our end in mind. When all is said and done, what do you want to have instilled within your loved ones? What lessons, traits, or wisdom do you want them to embody and carry on as an anchor for their life? More simply put, if your time came to a close today, can you answer this question: "Have I loved my family well?" That simple question is multi-faceted and filled with layers, but you know the answer right away. In our families, we leave 3 main legacies:

+ Emotional legacy
+ Social legacy
+ Spiritual legacy

Our emotional legacy consists of the confidence, support, identity, and unconditional love that they experience and know deeply in their hearts, beyond any shadow of doubt. Our social legacy consists of the values, responsibility, and guiding beliefs that help them navigate a successful and impactful life. Finally, our spiritual legacy consists of the examples we set to prioritize our spiritual life and relationship with God as an integral part of who we are.

As you reflect on these three areas, what is the legacy you desire to leave in those most important to you? Little of what they will carry on will be in words you have spoken. Rather, it will be modeled through the life you live. This is your true leadership legacy.

What is the legacy that I want to leave behind for my family?

Closing

This chapter may be sobering in some ways, as we all love deeply but may fall short of our own expectations at times. We all make mistakes in our journey to be who we want to be. But our hope is that this chapter encourages you to love your family and be present in ways you have always desired. When you close this book, look up, be present, pursue connection, and let your life be your love on display.

NEXT STEPS:

1. Who is in your "ground zero"? Who are those people that you are closest to? List their names out on a piece of paper and why you consider each of them a part of your closest relationships.

2. When listing out your family values, which value did you find rose to the top? Why is that one the most important to you and how will you ensure that it shows up in your life?

3. How did this chapter make you feel? What emotions did you find bubbling up and where do you think those came from? What adjustments, if any, can you make this week?

CHAPTER 10

The Role of Faith

John Maxwell so famously said, "Leadership is influence, nothing more, nothing less" (Maxwell, 1993, p. 1). We, too, believe that leading others is about living and giving fully to those around us in order to impact and influence their lives for the better. Although this whole leadership thing may not always seem easy, it is in fact quite simple in some ways.

Servant Leadership—It's All About People

As the two of us discussed the content and outline for this book, we established early on that we wanted to ensure that its foundations were rooted in our faith. As husbands, fathers, and leaders, we know that it is through God's grace and goodness that we have been given opportunities to lead and serve our families and organizations. When it comes to the greatest model of leadership, we look to Jesus and the impact He had here on earth. He lived a life of servant leadership and modeled what it truly means to lay down His life for the sake of others.

To this day, the model of servant leadership remains one of the foundations upon which Authentic Leadership Theory is built. The late Robert Greenleaf, noted for his work in the development of

Servant Leadership Theory, published an essay in 1970 depicting these characteristics of leading as a servant first:

"The servant leader is a servant first...Becoming a servant leader begins with the natural feeling that one wants to serve, to serve first. Then conscious choice brings one to aspire to lead. That person is sharply different from one who is a leader first.

The difference manifests itself in the care taken by the servant first to make sure that other people's highest priority needs are being served. The best test, and the most difficult to administer, is this: Do those served grow as persons? Do they, while being served, become healthier, wiser, freer, more autonomous, and more likely themselves to become servants?" (Greenleaf, 1970).

These words in fact reinforce much of the premise of this book. As we live and lead with authenticity and a heart for others, we have the ability to steward their growth into who they are capable of becoming. What an honor. It is from this place that we fully believe that loving those we lead truly matters. Not because they "earned" it, but because we are called to serve and love those around us. 1 John 4:19 says, "We love, because He first loved us."

Our Value System

A Story from Tyler

I remember finishing leading a staff meeting and someone walking up to me who said, "Sometimes when I hear you speak, it feels like I am sitting in church! You just don't mention God's name!"

Of course, this makes me chuckle, as it is not the first time someone has said something similar, in different leadership settings. This is because Kingdom principles are life-giving, hope-inducing, and peace-filling. When we talk about the characteristics of living and leading from our faith, we are literally talking about living from our values, loving those around us, honoring the greatness inside of others, confronting others in love, building in healthy support systems and accountability for our lives, living with purpose, and the list goes on.

These are not simply "great ideas" that leadership gurus have developed over the past fifty years. This is the value system of Heaven. These are ways we are called to live in community, grow each other as iron sharpens iron, and bring out the best in one another, all while living lives of character and humility.

A Story from Todd

One thing that is important to me as a leader is not shying away from sharing all the pieces of myself. My faith has never been something I have been ashamed of or afraid to share. In fact, there have been countless examples of me weaving my faith into the work that I do. Not in a way that is off-putting or shoving anything down anyone's throat. Yet in a way that is true to who I am.

The reality is when we share ourselves, all of ourselves, vulnerably and honestly, it allows others to walk alongside us and say, "Me, too."

My faith is an important part of who I am. It's at the basis of every decision that I make. As I connect with others and help them grow into who they're meant to be, I love learning about their own faiths and what grounds them.

We all have a guiding belief at our core. Though many of those close to me hold differing faiths they believe in, it doesn't change the way we are able to connect and grow together.

Our Source of Hope

There are most certainly challenging days in leadership. Days when it feels like the weight is too much to bear. Situations where you end up having to take responsibility for messes that you didn't make, but have to own. Or times when those you serve and lead are frustrated with you, even for illegitimate reasons. It is in these times that without hope and connection to our true source of peace, it would in fact be a bumpy ride. Leadership is hard because life is hard. No one ever said it would be easy. What God *did* promise, however, is strength for the journey.

Romans 8:28 says, *"And we know that in all things God works for the good of those who love Him, who have been called according to His purpose."* This verse has gotten us through more than one tough day. Because we know that there is peace available in the storm, there is hope in the midst of trials, and according to Romans 8:28, if it's not good, it's not over yet.

Our Model for Integrity

As we have taken a deep dive throughout this book into the necessity of establishing and living from our values, there is no greater model of integrity than Jesus. He lived and led from a place deeply rooted in His identity, and He was unwavering in the face of trials, distractions, and opportunities that could have otherwise deterred Him from His course. Life is not simply a series of things we are striving to say, "No" to, in order to live with character and integrity. Rather, it is about making the "Yes" to our calling and purpose in life *so big* that the rest simply pales in comparison. This is the significance of understanding our "Why."

We know that we are called to live a life set apart—one of integrity, values, and honor. In turn, we aim to model this in our teams that we lead, and most importantly in our families and children. This is a part of our legacy—both emotional and spiritual.

Humble Confidence

Let's be real: with leadership also comes the challenge of staying grounded in who we are—both with our actions and perspectives. That is why it is vital that we cultivate humility in our lives each day. In our friend Zac Bauermaster's 40 Day Devotional, *Leading with a Humble Heart,* he underscores the importance of staying rooted and grounded in who we are in Christ on a daily basis. At the start of his book, Zac encourages us to:

"Stare the challenges of leadership in the face through humility that can only be found in God's Word and prayer. By intentionally being in God's Word and prayer each day, God will not only equip us to face the challenges and test of leadership; but we will also learn to thrive in those moments and seasons as we operate from a place of humble confidence. *Humble enough to know that, apart from Christ, we can do nothing, and confident enough to know we can do all things through Christ"* (Bauermaster, 2022, p. xvii).

Our Identity

You have heard it through the pages of this book. Your value and identity are not defined by what you *do.* Your title and achievements aren't meant to validate your identity as a status symbol for success. And on the flip side, when things go sideways, it does not mean who you are is a failure. The fact of the matter is many people subconsciously associate what they do with who they are. It might sound silly for us to say it out loud, because deep down we know it shouldn't be the case. But our thoughts and feelings can oftentimes work against us and try to tell us otherwise. They can control us if we aren't careful.

The truth is, our identity is only found in God. We are fully loved and fully accepted, not because of what we do, but because of who He is. He is pleased with us, and is passionate about us walking in the fullness that He has called us to in our life. He loves us in spite of our choices and our mistakes.

This is not a free pass to say, "God loves me fully, so it doesn't matter what I do," but rather it is, "He has designed me for greatness, and I will commit my life to growing into the person I have been created to be." Knowing our identity is actually a call to greatness. One that we renew our mind to and pursue with our whole hearts each and every day.

Leadership and Faith in Today's World

We are unashamed in our faith and recognize that by God's grace we are saved and by His goodness that we even have the opportunity to write these pages. We also both lead in settings that are in the public sector, and know that living out our faith looks a certain way when it comes to public education, the business world, non-profit sector, etc.

If you take anything from the pages in this chapter, we hope you will connect the dots that living out your faith is simply your life on display. The life that you live, the interactions that you have, the way you love those around you, the way you serve others—every bit communicates a message of who you are and the faith you live by. Your actions will speak far louder than your words ever will. How do you treat those that can do nothing for you? How do you address and confront others in love who may have hurt you? How is your integrity and character on display in the calm *and* the stormy seas? How do you react around those who have beliefs that differ from yours?

This is our hope and prayer for you. That as you build authenticity in your life, you will actually reveal the very nature of who you are and who God is in your life. Let the life you live and the way you lead be your testimony.

NEXT STEPS:

1. Where does your source of hope come from? Take a moment to reflect on your journey. Where did it start? How has it evolved? And where do you find yourself now? More specifically, how does it show up in the way you live and lead?

CHAPTER 11

~

You Have What It Takes

When the Going Gets Tough

We have all been there. Times when we simply feel downtrodden. Times when we feel overwhelmed to the point where we question if we have what it takes to continue on. Times when we actually begin to doubt our own ability or potential to come out victorious on the other side. Where we feel like it's time to pack it in and walk away. That someone else can do a far better job than what we're doing.

These crossroads in life which are inevitably experienced by every single one of us, are *defining moments*. They are bigger and represent more than simply the current situation that we are in. They are the building blocks upon which we develop resilience, cultivate perseverance, and fortify who we are and what we believe about ourselves. They are—opportunities.

As much as that sounded like it could have been heard on the front lines of a battle scene in *Braveheart*, that word, *resilience*, is a pivotal characteristic of those who live authentic, powerful, and healthy lives. Not *powerful* in the sense of title or influence or social stature, but *powerfully* in charge of our response to adversity by understanding that we can either be victims to our situation and circumstance, or we can rise above in our perspective and response. It is our *response* to adversity, not the adversity itself that determines our outcomes in life.

The Cost of Authenticity

Like most things in life, anything of value comes at a cost. If you desire to pursue greater levels of your education, it takes time, money, and focus. If you desire to invest and grow in your marriage, it takes humility, patience, and sacrifice. If you want to become the father or mother you have always desired to be, it takes patience, forgiveness, and unconditional love. And if you desire to live and lead with authenticity, it takes integrity, resilience, and unwavering commitment to that vision.

This chapter in many ways brings a crescendo to many of the traits and processes that we have discussed that build authenticity in our lives. However, just as stated before, authenticity is not a fixed point in our lives, but rather a journey and process that we commit to daily. Which means, along the way there will be days when it will be easy, and days when it will be difficult. Days when we feel like we might be starting over again completely. However, difficulty does not mean we are failing; it means we are presented with opportunities to grow and move forward. It is all about our perspective.

> **Insight from a fellow leader:** *"I work to be an authentic leader by continuing to discipline myself to align my intentions with my actions each day that are aligned with my values. To care deeply enough about others that I not only share specifically the good I see in them, but also care enough to give specific feedback. High accountability and support."*
> –John Norlin, Co-Founder of CharacterStrong

The Value of Self-Discipline

We are made up of a sum of our beliefs, habits, and behaviors. However, if we are not intentional in identifying *who* we desire to be and *how* we are going to get there, we leave much of that to chance.

Self-discipline is the ability to keep pushing yourself forward and taking action toward those desired outcomes in your life, whatever they may be. It's the unbreakable determination to keep doing what you should be doing, no matter what obstacles, opportunities, or distractions appear on your journey. This includes saying no to the *good* in order to say yes to the *great*. However, self-discipline is different from motivation or willpower because it is the unwavering *commitment* to show up every day and do the work. Without self-discipline, motivation, and willpower, we will eventually burnout. As Jack Canfield so well puts it, "Self-discipline is the consistent practice of chopping wood to fuel the fire every single day, no matter how tired or busy you are, or what the weather is like" (Canfield, 2022).

Why is this important to building authenticity? Because without self-discipline and resolute commitment to our values, integrity, relationships, and priorities, we can get so easily tossed in the waves of our responsibilities of life and the challenges that derail us. Then, we are left with the "idea" of who we desire to be but lack the strategy and muscle memory to get back on track.

What are the little things that you need to build into your life so that you can grow into who you desire to be? What is your "firewood" that you need to chop every day, no matter how busy or tired you are, or what the weather is like? Start small. Build on your wins. Have grace for yourself when you fail. And stay steadfast when adversity tries to distract you. You've got this.

Positive Psychological Capital: A Deeper Look

In Chapter 2, we discussed Positive Psychological Capital as a byproduct of authentic leadership. These core tenets of *hope, optimism, self-efficacy, and resilience* are attributes that are developed in oneself through intentionality and daily inner work. In fact, although each of them is unique in their own way, they are powerfully interwoven as a foundation for our *thought lives* and a difference maker in the way we respond to adversity and challenges.

When we cultivate *hope*, we are willing to look fear and doubt in the face and expect a favorable outcome instead. This means that although there are trials in front of us, things *will* work out for good in the end. Low-hope people avoid problems, focus on symptoms, feed their fear, get tired, and give up. However, high-hope people engage in problem solving, focus on solutions, feed their faith, get inspired, and refuse to quit.

Furthermore, *optimism* isn't the denial of the current state that you are in. Rather, it is the belief that there are clearer waters ahead. As the old saying goes, "A pessimist sees the difficulty in every opportunity; an optimist sees the opportunity in every difficulty."

Self-efficacy refers to one's confidence in their ability to complete a task or achieve a goal. It is the inner belief that says, "I have what it takes." Research shows that it is deeply tied to the actual belief system we have about ourselves. When the battle arises, do you see yourself with a sword or running for the hills? And if you don't like what you see, how can you change it?

Finally, *resilience* refers to that indefinable quality that allows some people to be knocked down by life's adversities and come back stronger than ever. Rather than letting obstacles overcome them and being defined by disappointment, they embrace the challenge, get back up, and keep moving forward.

While on the journey of building authenticity in your life, your thoughts matter. Your belief system about yourself matters. And your perspective really matters. You have a choice to simply *manage* your life through your situations, or you can stand tall in the midst of it, knowing that you have an opportunity to learn, grow, and *overcome*.

> **Insight from a fellow leader:** *"I do want people to always see me as "strong," but it's also important for them to know that I don't have all the answers. I have areas, both professionally and personally, that are in need of help/support. When people know that about you, it helps them to see your commonality. You have flaws like they do, which then in turn helps build a stronger bond and trust when you're in a leadership position."*
> –Jackie Powell, K-5 Reading Interventionist

When the Storm Comes

One of the most powerful and respected creatures in the animal kingdom is the Bald Eagle. Known for their vision, fearlessness, and tenacity, they are a symbol of freedom and strength. One of the most incredible attributes of the eagle is actually their response to adversity and storms. Unlike nearly every other bird that seeks shelter as the storm comes, the eagle flies directly at the storm. As it flies straight into the storm, it embraces the turbulence and actively engages the stronger winds to push itself above the storm clouds, where it can then soar in clear skies. Rather than flying down for shelter to wait out the storm, it rises up and faces it head on.

As a leader and in life, we come up against our fair share of storms. However, our trials do not define us. What they do however, is reveal what is inside of us. How do we respond when the storm comes? Do we face the storm head on? Do we complain that it is yet *another* storm in our life? Do we hunker down and wait for it to pass? Do we *blame others* for the storm in our lives? Do we look for someone else to *rescue* us and then become bitter when no one does? Do we just give up? We will never be able to control and mitigate every storm from coming our way—but what we *can* control is how we *respond* to it.

A Story from Todd

From a young age I've always felt a pull that I was destined for more. Though I never quite knew what that meant. I found myself embracing the moments of life that I had been placed into, yet still yearning for what's next. It's funny, though, that as we grow out of our adolescent years, our doubt and insecurity begin to creep their way inside. Sometimes we ourselves allow them to walk right through the front doors of our minds. Yet other times it's like someone we know, we trusted, beat down the door and just threw doubt and insecurity on us.

All throughout high school I served on our student council. I remember running for office year after year and getting elected as a class representative. I attended every meeting and volunteered constantly because I wanted to make a difference on my campus and in my community, and I just knew this was how I could do it. When I was a senior in high school I decided I wanted to do more. So I made the choice to run for Senior Class President. It was an exciting time as I created posters, made stickers, and organized a campaign.

But I'll never forget what happened next. Forty-five minutes before we were to head to the gym to give our speeches in front of our entire class, my teacher received a phone call on her classroom phone. She hung up and let me know that the principal needed to see me in his office.

Immediately I went into panic mode. You must understand something here. I was NEVER in trouble in school. I got good grades, completed all my work, served at my church and on countless volunteer committees. Plus, my mom would have whipped my behind in front of everyone if I ever embarrassed her. So as you can probably guess, I had never been called to the principal's office before. I quickly made my way down to the principal's office and found my principal sitting behind his desk with the head assistant principal standing next to him. They called me in and asked me to sit down. Shaking, I took a seat.

The next fifteen minutes are somewhat of a blur. There are parts I remember clear as day and others that remain a little fuzzy. Due to a misunderstanding on their end, they berated and scolded me. What was said has stuck with me since that day. I can clearly remember the principal saying, "We don't need or want leaders like you on our campus."

I'd love to say that conversation (and that day in general) didn't bother me. But to this very day, I still find doubt creeping in, and I start believing that the world doesn't need or want a leader like me.

I share this story as a reminder that deep inside me I know I'm made to make a difference, to leave a legacy. And I believe with every fiber of my being that you were also created to impact the lives of others. There will always be people who make us feel less than, unworthy, or more. But you can't let them steal your purpose. When we rise through the struggles we're able to lead even more authentically.

Why We Need Trials in Our Lives

That's right, you read that correctly. As uncomfortable as they are, and as messy as they feel, trials can actually play a beneficial role in our lives. Without trials, we miss the opportunity to be forged in the fire, and refined into a better version of ourselves. Singer-songwriter Nichole Nordeman wrote, "How would I know the morning, if I knew not midnight?" (Nordeman, 2017). Although our first instinct is often self-preservation and avoiding the pain of trials in our lives, there are lessons to be learned, perseverance to grow, and character to be refined. So, we will dare to say it: don't let your trials and opportunities go to waste.

Martin Luther King Jr. said, "The ultimate measure of a man is not where he stands in moments of comfort and convenience, but where he stands at times of challenge and controversy" (King, 1963). This is where your values are put to the test. The character that you possess and how you respond during times of hardship will be what your team will remember in times of success. This is the same for every aspect of our lives—our marriage, our work, and our families.

When we are going through a trial in life, think of it as an opportunity to learn. Say to yourself, "OK, what can this teach me?" When we assume a posture of humility and a growth mindset, the likelihood of success increases, because our perspective changes. We no longer are the chicken hunkered down waiting for the storm to pass, but rather we are the eagle facing it head on. As a result, if we are able to pinpoint the emotions, feelings, and tendencies that overwhelm us in the midst of the trial and are willing to process through them, the next time we face a similar situation we are better equipped and prepared to overcome and prosper. Overcoming trials builds momentum and maturity in our lives.

Hellen Keller once said, "Be of good cheer. Do not think of today's failures, but of the success that may come tomorrow. You have set yourselves a difficult task, but you will succeed if you persevere, and you will find joy in overcoming obstacles. Remember, no effort that we

> Embracing our trials as opportunities for growth builds momentum and maturity in our lives.

make to attain something beautiful is ever lost" (Keller, n.d.). What a perspective in the midst of difficulty!

Guard Your Heart

This is a gritty chapter, no doubt. We discussed everything from the inevitable challenges we face in life and leadership, to the sacrifice that it takes to stay true to the course even when we feel like throwing in the towel. Be it disappointments or difficulties, celebrations or victories, it is important that we make sure we are aware of our *internal* responses, because they will last far beyond the actual situation. When the challenge knocks on your door, will you end up bitter or better as a result?

Unfortunately, we have known some leaders who were well-intended and sincere in their hearts to lead others well. However, throughout time, they became calloused from their experiences, and cynical in their perspective. They became jaded towards people's intentions, and found it difficult to see the best in those around them. They disconnected emotionally from those they led because their hearts had hardened. You can probably picture someone in your own life experience as well.

This isn't meant to be dramatic by any sense, and in fact this is more of a subtle slide than we realize. *You* might in fact even be able to relate to this in some way. If that is the case, it is OK. This is why you are reading this book. To go deeper, to look inward, and build true authenticity as a leader. Leave no stone unturned as you develop into the person and leader you desire to be.

This subtle slide is one that is a result of not processing our pain and disappointment in life in a healthy way, right away, and with the support of those we trust. When we are let down or betrayed, we have a crossroads moment of forgiving, addressing, and growing, *or* not processing through it and harboring unforgiveness. Each response plants a different seed in our hearts, and each subsequent life experience confirms either of those feelings and waters that specific seed.

Metaphors aside, as leaders it is vital that we process through our feelings and live from a powerful place that sees the best in people, even in their mess, and extends forgiveness to others when they fall short and hurt us as a result. Leadership is a heavy responsibility, and one that gets heavier if not carried the right way. This underscores the importance of having healthy support systems in place for you to process with, get honest feedback from, and to encourage you to live and lead from a healthy place. As the Proverb says, "Guard your heart above all else, for out of it flows the springs of life."

The Man In The Arena

Many of you are familiar with Theodore Roosevelt's speech from August, 1910 (Roosevelt, 1910). In life, we will most certainly face trials that knock us down. But it is in our willingness to get back up that defines who we are. Your willingness to pick up this book. Your willingness to show up every day for your family. Your willingness to humble yourself to receive feedback from others. And your willingness to see the gold inside of every person you lead. Your willingness to keep going. These things will leave a greater legacy than you realize. Will you stumble? Yes. But as you get up and wipe off the dust, know that your cause is indeed worth it.

> "It is not the critic who counts; not the man who points out how the strong man stumbles, or where the doer of deeds could have done them better. The credit belongs to the man who is actually in the arena, whose face is marred by dust and sweat and blood; who strives valiantly; who errs, who comes short again and again, because there is no effort without error and shortcoming; but who does actually strive to do the deeds; who knows great enthusiasms, the great devotions;

who spends himself in a worthy cause; who at the best knows in the end the triumph of high achievement, and who at the worst, if he fails, at least fails while daring greatly, so that his place shall never be with those cold and timid souls who neither know victory nor defeat" (Roosevelt, 1910).

NEXT STEPS:

1. You've gotten this far in the book! As you make changes in your life and build authenticity, the storms, the doubt, and the insecurities will try to creep in. After reading this far, what do you find yourself still battling?

2. How can you utilize the strategies and blueprint of this book to pursue authenticity and growth?

CHAPTER 12

~

What Comes Next?

If you have read this far, it says more about you than it does about the content of this book. It says that you are committed to living and leading fully from who you really are meant to be. Too often in life, we hold ourselves back because of our own limiting beliefs, mindsets, fears, or insecurities. There are even times when we find false comfort and security in them. We use them to reinforce our behaviors and actions, or lack thereof. We allow them to control us.

But today is a new day. Today is your opportunity to reflect on the honest conversations you have had with yourself throughout this book, and begin to apply them day by day. To revisit this book again when necessary. Remember, building authenticity is a life process. It is not a life event. It takes courage, humility, vulnerability, and is not meant to be done alone.

Write down your values so that you can reflect on them daily. Have them engraved so deeply in your mind and heart that they are the lens through which every decision is made.

Spend time each day fostering self-awareness and self-reflection, so that you can course-correct yourself when it is needed so that you stay true to not only yourself, but your vision for your life.

Invite people into your life who love you and are willing to speak to your blind spots. Pull back the veil of your insecurities or even ways you simply desire to grow, and trust those people to support you. They will, because they love you and want what is best for you. You can't do this without them.

Be keenly aware each day of your schedule and the way your priorities are showing up. Are you scheduling your priorities, or are you merely prioritizing your schedule? There is a difference. Create your life by design so that you are giving your best to what matters most.

As you stand in front of those you lead, remember that you have been given the gift to speak into their life, call out the greatness, and empower them to grow. If not you, then who? Never take the gift of leadership for granted. You're exactly where you were meant to be.

Every time you walk through the front doors of your home, remember that this is your most important leadership responsibility. There is no replacement for you in your home. Love well, be present, and leave the legacy you desire. They need you.

Stay grounded in your faith. Know that we can do nothing significant in this life apart from He who created us. Do nothing in your own strength, but in all things trust in the Lord, and He will direct your paths. In His eyes, you are worthy.

Finally, be courageous. You have what it takes. Living a life of authenticity in pursuit of your fullest potential is not easy. If it were easy, everyone would do it. But you were made for greatness. And you know that inside of you is the potential to impact your world around you in a way that changes lives forever. This is the path of building authenticity. So, pick up that hammer, grab those nails, and keep building.

References

Atkins, R. (2006). Watching you [Recorded by Rodney Atkins]. On *If you're going through hell*. Curb Records.

Avey, J. B., Reichard, R. J., Luthans, F., Mhatre, K. H. (2011). Meta-analysis of the impact of positive psychological capital on employee attitudes, behaviors and performance. *Human Resource Development Quarterly, 22*(2), 127–152.

Avolio, B. J. (2005). *Leadership development in balance: Made/born.* Mahwah, NJ: Lawrence Earlbaum Associates.

Avolio, B. J., Gardner, W. L., Walumbwa, F. O., Luthans, F., & May, D.R. (2004). Unlocking the mask: A look at the process by which authentic leaders impact follower attitudes and behaviors. *The leadership quarterly, 15*(1), 801-823.

Bauermaster, Z. (2022). *Leading with a humble heart: A 40 day devotional for leaders.* Hanover, PA: ConnectEDD Publishing.

Brown, B. (2012). *Daring greatly: How the courage to be vulnerable transforms the way we live, love, parent, and lead.* New York: Avery.

Canfield, J. (2022). *What is self-discipline? 7 ways to develop it.* Jack Canfield: Maximizing Your Potential. https://jackcanfield.com/blog/what-is-self-discipline/

Casas, J. (2017). *Culturize: Every student. Every day. Whatever it takes.* Dave Burgess Consulting, Inc.

Cathy, T. (2015). *How do you know if a man or woman needs encouragement? They are breathing.* Facebook. https://www.facebook.com/ChickfilA/photos/truett-cathy-was-fond-of-saying-how-do-you-know-if-someone-needs-encouragement-i/10153849973195101/

Clapp-Smith, R., Vogelsang, G.R., Avey, J.B. (2009). Authentic leadership and positive psychological capital. *Journal of leadership and organizational studies, 15*(3), 227-239.

Clear, James. [@JamesClear]. (2022, September 26). *If you keep doing what you are about to do today for the next five years, will you end up with more of what you want or less of what you want?* Twitter. https://twitter.com/JamesClear/status/1574398386060419073

Cook, Tyler P. (2020). *The development of authentic leadership from K-12 principals' perspectives.* (Doctoral dissertation, Point Park University.) Proquest Dissertations and Theses Global.

Covey, S. R. (2013, January 25). Leadership is a choice, not a position. *Business Standard.* https://www.business-standard.com/article/management/leadership-is-a-choice-not-a-position-stepen-r-covey-109020300076_1.html

Cunnington, H. (2020). *I do boundaries: A Bible study to discover your boundaries, protect what matters, and stop feeling bad about it.* Havilah Cunnington.

Dweck, C.S. (2006). *Mindset.* New York: Random House.

Edelman. (2022). *2022 Edelman Trust Barometer.* https://www.edelman.com/trust/2022-trust-barometer

REFERENCES

Fortune. (2014, March 20). The World's 50 Greatest Leaders (2014). https://fortune.com/2014/03/20/worlds-50-greatest-leaders/

Gardner, W.L., Avolio, B.J., Luthans, F., May, D.R., Walumbwa, F. (2005). "Can you see the real me?" A self-based model of authentic leader and follower development. *The leadership quarterly, 16*(3), 343-372.
George, B. (2015). *Discover your true north: Becoming an authentic leader.* Hoboken, NJ: Wiley.

George, B., & Sims, P. (2007). *True north: Discover your authentic leadership.* San Francisco, CA: Jossey-Bass.

George, W., Sims, P., McLean, A.N., Mayer, D. (2007). Discovering your authentic leadership. *Harvard business review,* 1-8.

Goleman, D., Boyatzis, R., McKee, A. (2002). *Primal leadership: Realizing the power of emotional intelligence.* Boston: Harvard Business School Press.

Goodreads. (n.d.) A quote by Hellen Keller. Goodreads. Retrieved December 27, 2022, from https://www.goodreads.com/quotes/130061-be-of-good-cheer-do-not-think-of-today-s-failures

Greenleaf, R. K. (1970). *The servant as a leader.* Robert K. Greenleaf Center for Servant Leadership. https://www.greenleaf.org/what-is-servant-leadership/

Groeschel, C. (Host). (2018, August 1). Creating an empowering culture, part 2 (No. 17). In *Craig Groeschel Leadership Podcast.* Life. Church. https://www.life.church/leadershippodcast/creating-an-empowering-culture-part-2/

Ilies, R., Morgeson, F. P., & Nahrgang, J. D. (2005). Authentic leadership and eudemonic well-being: Understanding leader-follower outcomes. *The Leadership Quarterly, 16*(3), 373–394.

Johnson, Bill. (2011, May 15). *If you don't live by the praises of men, you won't die by their criticism.* Facebook. https://www.facebook.com/BillJohnson-Ministries/posts/if-you-dont-live-by-the-praises-of-men-you-wont-die-by-their-criticisms/10150181003393387/

Kernis, M. H. (2003). Toward a conceptualization of optimal self-esteem. *Psychological inquiry, 14*(1), 1–26.

King Jr., M. L. (1963). *Strength to love.* Harper & Row.

Luft, J., & Ingham, H. (1955). The johari window, a graphic model of inter-personal awareness. *Proceedings of the Western Training Laboratory in Group Development,* 246, 2014-03.

Luthans, F. & Avolio, B.J. (2003). Authentic leadership development. *Positive organizational scholarship,* 241-261. San Francisco: Barret-Koehler.

Maxwell, J. C. (1993). *Developing the leader within you.* Nashville, TN: Thomas Nelson, Inc.

Maxwell, J. C. (Host). (2022, May 4). Leading with gratitude. In *The John Maxwell leadership podcast.* The John Maxwell Company. https://johnmax-wellleadershippodcast.com/episodes/john-maxwell-leading-with-gratitude

Merriam-Webster. (2022). *Potential.* https://www.merriam-webster.com/dictionary/potential

Nordeman, N. (2017). Sunrise [Recorded by Nicole Nordeman]. On *Recollection - The best of Nicole Nordeman.* Sparrow Records.

Roosevelt, T. (1910, April 23). Citizenship in a Republic. [Speech at the Sorbonne, Paris]. https://www.theodorerooseveltcenter.org/Learn-About-TR/TR-Encyclopedia/Culture-and-Society/Man-in-the-Arena.aspx

REFERENCES

Silk, D. (2009). *Culture of honor.* Shippensburg, PA: Destiny Image.

Sinek, Simon. (2019, January 30). *Great leaders don't blame the tools they are given. They work to sharpen them.* Facebook. https://www.facebook.com/simonsinek/posts/great-leaders-dont-blame-the-tools-they-are-given-they-work-to-sharpen-them/10157029040281499/

Walumbwa, F. O., Avolio, B. J., Gardner, W. L., Wernsing, T. S., & Peterson, S. J. (2008). Authentic leadership: Development and validation of a theory-based measure. *Journal of management, 34*(1), 89-126.

About the Authors

Todd Nesloney is the Director of Culture and Strategic Leadership for the Texas Elementary Principals and Supervisors Association (TEPSA). In addition to his work at TEPSA he is also the Director of Lead On (under the Get Your Teach On umbrella). He has also served as an award-winning principal of a PreK-5th Grade campus of over 775 students in a rural town in Texas. He has been recognized by the White House, John C Maxwell, the Center for Digital Education, National School Board Association, the BAMMYS, and more for his work in education and with children. Todd has written five books, including *Kids Deserve It, Stories From Webb, Sparks in the Dark, When Kids Lead* and *In This Season: Words for the Heart.* He also released his first children's book *Spruce and Lucy.* He is passionate about doing whatever it takes for our students and helping others tell their story. He lives in Brenham, Texas with his wife Lissette and their twin boys Liam and Brixton. Connect with Todd on his website at www.toddnesloney. com.

Dr. Tyler Cook is the Principal of Klein Elementary School in the Harbor Creek School District located in Erie, Pennsylvania. In addition to his work in educational leadership, Tyler serves as the Executive Director of Lake Erie Church. He holds his Doctorate in Leadership and Administration from Point Park University, where he focused his dissertation research on Authentic Leadership development. Tyler is passionate about developing high-impact leaders who will grow their organizations, staff, or students into their fullest potential. From fostering healthy cultures to empowering others to lead, Tyler believes that there is greatness inside of every person, and it is the privilege of leaders to unlock it. Tyler lives in Erie, Pennsylvania with his wife Stacey and their four children: Elijah, Judah, Noah, and Anna. Connect with Tyler on his website at www.drtylercook.com.

More from
ConnectEDD Publishing

Since 2015, ConnectEDD has worked to transform education by empowering educators to become better-equipped to teach, learn, and lead. What started as a small company designed to provide professional learning events for educators has grown to include a variety of services to help educators and administrators address essential challenges. ConnectEDD offers instructional and leadership coaching, professional development workshops focusing on a variety of educational topics, a roster of nationally recognized educator associates who possess hands-on knowledge and experience, educational conferences custom-designed to meet the specific needs of schools, districts, and state/national organizations, and ongoing, personalized support, both virtually and onsite. In 2020, ConnectEDD expanded to include publishing services designed to provide busy educators with books and resources consisting of practical information on a wide variety of teaching, learning, and leadership topics. Please visit us online at connecteddpublishing.com or contact us at: info@connecteddpublishing.com

Recent Publications:

Live Your Excellence: Action Guide by Jimmy Casas
Culturize: Action Guide by Jimmy Casas
Daily Inspiration for Educators: Positive Thoughts for Every Day of the Year

by Jimmy Casas

Eyes on Culture: Multiply Excellence in Your School by Emily Paschall

Pause. Breathe. Flourish. Living Your Best Life as an Educator by William D. Parker

L.E.A.R.N.E.R. Finding the True, Good, and Beautiful in Education by Marita Diffenbaugh

Educator Reflection Tips Volume II: Refining Our Practice by Jami Fowler-White

Handle With Care: Managing Difficult Situations in Schools with Dignity and Respect by Jimmy Casas and Joy Kelly

Disruptive Thinking: Preparing Learners for Their Future by Eric Sheninger

Permission to be Great: Increasing Engagement in Your School by Dan Butler

Daily Inspiration for Educators: Positive Thoughts for Every Day of the Year, *Volume II* by Jimmy Casas

The 6 Literacy Levers: Creating a Community of Readers by Brad Gustafson

The Educator's ATLAS: Your Roadmap to Engagement by Weston Kieschnick

In This Season: Words for the Heart by Todd Nesloney, LaNesha Tabb, Tanner Olson, and Alice Lee

Leading with a Humble Heart: A 40-Day Devotional for Leaders by Zac Bauermaster

Recalibrate the Culture: Our Why...Our Work...Our Values by Jimmy Casas

Creating Curious Classrooms: The Beauty of Questions by Emma Chiappetta

Crafting the Culture: 45 Reflections on What Matters Most by Joe Sanfelippo and Jeffrey Zoul

Improving School Mental Health: The Thriving School Community Solution by Charle Peck and Dr. Cameron Caswell